Virtual Schooling

Issues in the Development of E-Learning Policy

Edited by
Donovan R. Walling

Foreword by
John F. (Jack) Jennings

Phi Delta Kappa Educational Foundation
Bloomington, Indiana U.S.A.

Cover design by
Victoria Voelker

Phi Delta Kappa Educational Foundation
408 North Union Street
Post Office Box 789
Bloomington, IN 47402-0789
U.S.A.

Printed in the United States of America

Library of Congress Catalog Card Number 2003103874
ISBN 0-87367-847-8

Table of Contents

PART I
From Distance Education to Virtual Schooling

PART II
E-Learning Policy and Practicality Come of Age

Foreword

Preserving Principles of Public Education in an Online World: What Policy Makers Should Be Asking About Virtual Schools

John F. (Jack) Jennings

Director of the Center on Education Policy

Virtual schools — education organizations that offer courses through the Internet — are rapidly becoming part of the landscape of American education. Largely unknown a decade ago, the phenomenon of online education for secondary, middle, and even elementary school students has been fueled by the growth of computers and Internet access in both schools and homes. States, local school districts, regional consortia, higher education institutions, nonprofit organizations, and private vendors today offer a smorgasbord of courses and services, many of which are organized into entities called "schools." These virtual schools include many of the basic components found in "face-to-face" education, including teachers, administrators, and guidance counselors; textbooks, schedules, and course assignments; and other instructional resources.

Preserving Long-Held Principles in a Virtual World

Most policy discussions about virtual schools focus on how this new mode of education is changing the delivery, structure, governance, and funding of education. Less attention is paid to how these changes could affect the deeper purposes and principles underlying a system of public education — in other words, the expectations and ideals that have shaped the American vision of public education for more than a century. These include such purposes as preparing students for life, work, and citizenship and creating a cohesive society; and such principles as providing universal access and equity in education and making schools responsive to their local community.

Virtual education is a prime example of a fast-moving trend that could have a major effect on these purposes and principles. Virtual schools are calling into question longstanding ideas about the definition of a public school, the social goals of public education, and local control of public education.

As an independent national advocate for effective public schools, the Center on Education Policy (CEP) encourages policy makers to have an *explicit* conversation about how virtual schools — or any other far-reaching education reform — will affect the fundamental purposes and principles of public education. CEP supports changes that will help students learn better, but we also believe that these changes should be implemented with full awareness of their effect on fundamental principles. This kind of dialogue will help policy makers determine which purposes and principles are worth keeping; and it will help policy makers preserve these purposes and principles, even in the midst of dramatic change.

To stimulate these types of conversations, CEP has generated a set of key questions that policy makers should ask about major education reforms. These questions are grouped according to a list of six essential purposes and principles of public education developed by CEP after talking with many citizens.

Key Questions that Policy Makers Should Ask About Education Reforms

Effective preparation for life, work, and citizenship. Will the proposed reform produce an education of the quality needed to effectively prepare young people: 1) to lead fulfilling and con-tributing lives, 2) to be productively employed, and 3) to be responsible citizens in a democratic society?

Social cohesion and shared culture. Will the proposed reform promote a cohesive American society by bringing together chil-dren from diverse backgrounds and encouraging them to get along? Will it help to form a shared American culture and to transmit democratic values?

Universal access and free cost. Will the proposed reform guar-antee a public education that is universally accessible to all children within the governing jurisdiction and is free of charge to parents and students?

Equity and nondiscrimination. Will the proposed reform pro-vide the same quality of education for poor children as for those who are not poor? Will it treat all children justly and without dis-crimination based on race, ethnicity, gender, disability, religious affiliation, or economic status?

Public accountability and responsiveness. Will the proposed reform ensure that education supported with public dollars re-mains accountable to taxpayers and the public authorities that represent them? Will the reform be responsive to the needs of local communities and afford citizens a voice in the governance of their schools?

Religious neutrality. Will the proposed reform provide a pub-lic education that is religiously neutral and respectful of religious freedom?

Major Findings

In April 2002 the Center on Education Policy held a conference on virtual schools. Three main findings emerged from that meet-ing and from the center's analysis of other research on virtual schools:

- Virtual schools are an important tool for expanding oppor-tunities in public education if states implement them care-fully, effectively, and equitably.

- Virtual schools should serve as a supplement to and not a replacement for a comprehensive public school education. In the future, as needs change, technologies offer more flexibility, and educators gain more experience and evaluation data from virtual schooling, policy makers could reconsider whether virtual schools could provide a comprehensive education in some situations.
- Virtual schools funded with public money should be held accountable to the same broad principles and policies as other forms of public education in such areas as academic outcomes, equity, and religious neutrality. But in such areas as attendance, scheduling, and funding formulas, states will probably need to revise existing policies to make them workable for virtual schools.

Recommendations

The Center on Education Policy has developed several recommendations to help state and national policy makers create, support, and regulate K-12 virtual schools in ways that will maintain the essential purposes and principles of public education. The report* on which this foreword is based contains a fuller discussion of the issues underlying these recommendations and examples of promising practices.

Effective Preparation for Life, Work, and Citizenship
Policy makers should develop clear indicators for evaluating the quality of online education. Some of these indicators should be much the same as those used for traditional schools, such as student academic achievement, alignment of course content with state standards, course completion rates, and teacher qualifica-

---

*A copy of the report, *Preserving Principles of Public Education in an Online World: What Policy Makers Should Be Asking About Virtual Schools*, is available from the Center on Education Policy, 1001 Connecticut Avenue, N.W., Suite 522, Washington, D.C. 20036. Phone (202) 822-8065. The report may be downloaded free of charge at the CEP website: www.CEP-DC.org.

tions. Others should be specific to online education, such as interactivity in course design, reliability of technology and technical support, and teachers' ability to teach in an online environment.

Social Cohesion and Shared Culture

Policy makers should insist on frequent, regular, and timely interaction among online students, between online teachers and students, and with facilitators or onsite mentors in the home school to enhance student learning and social interaction.

To ensure that virtual education supplements but does not supplant a comprehensive public education experience, state or local administrators should set a maximum number of online courses a student can take in a semester or overall to meet graduation requirements.

Universal Access and Free Cost

Policy makers should take aggressive steps to ensure that all public school students have equal access to online courses. This should include covering the cost of online courses for low-income students and making available home computers, modems, and Internet access to low-income families.

States, school districts, and Web-based course developers should make sure that course content, designs, and tools meet federal accessibility standards for students with learning or other disabilities.

State policies should protect public school districts from losing funds to virtual charter schools or from having to pay for the participation of private or home-schooled children they would otherwise not be supporting. States that choose to include home-schooled children in publicly funded virtual schools should provide separate funding for this purpose.

Equity and Nondiscrimination

Policy makers should develop guidelines and safeguards to ensure equitable online learning opportunities for all public school students, not just those who are taking advanced courses or are skilled technology users. States and school districts should provide all students with the supports and technology skills necessary to learn online.

When developing new courses or selecting existing courses to offer, policy makers should target resources on subjects that serve the greatest number of students or the students with the greatest need of assistance.

Policy makers should take care not to allow virtual schooling to become a watered-down way to address persistent teacher shortages in schools serving low-income, minority, or rural students.

Public Accountability and Responsiveness

Virtual schools that receive public money should be accountable to and overseen by public authorities, such as states or local school districts.

Parents and citizens should have input into policy decisions that affect the availability, operation, and funding of virtual schools in their communities. States and school districts should make public the average test scores, other student outcomes, and evaluation reports for all virtual schools.

Religious Neutrality

Virtual schools that receive public funds should be held to the same principles of religious neutrality and respect for religious freedom as are traditional public schools, such as prohibiting course content that endorses a particular religion.

This Book

The conference that CEP held on virtual schools led to the publication of this book. Donovan Walling, director of publications and research for Phi Delta Kappa International, attended the meeting and became convinced that the issues surrounding virtual schools needed to be more fully understood in the education community. Most of the authors of the articles that follow also attended the conference and so agreed to contribute their expertise to this volume.

We urge you, when reading their articles, to recall the principles underlying public education and the recommendations that flowed from the work of the conference and our own research. Virtual schools hold great promise to improve education, but we must attend to how we structure this exciting new enterprise so that its potential will be realized.

Introduction

In 2002 the Washington, D.C.-based Center on Education Policy held a symposium titled "Virtual High Schools: Changing Schools, Enduring Principles." The purpose of the symposium was to examine some of the salient policy issues that surround virtual schooling. Most of the writers in this volume participated in the symposium, as Jack Jennings indicates in his foreword, "Preserving Principles of Public Education in an Online World."

The purpose of this book is to extend and enlarge the dialogue on policy issues related to e-learning. It is timely because virtual schools are proliferating and likely will continue to do so for the foreseeable future. The writers in this collection of essays have studied the issues; several have direct experience with virtual schools. All are concerned that schools of every sort, including virtual schools, offer students the best possible education.

The essays are divided into two sections. Part I, From Distance Education to Virtual Schooling, offers background. Virtual schooling has its roots in distance education, and so it seems appropriate to ground this collection with two historical pieces, both first published relatively recently, in 1998, but "historical" nonetheless, given the pace of technological change. The first is "Distance Education and Tomorrow's Students," by Barbara L. Ludlow and Michael C. Duff. These authors define distance education and offer a perspective on trends, possibilities, and problems associated with distance education. They also consider technologies and their applications in elementary and secondary education. The second essay is "Distance Education, Electronic Networking, and School Policy," by Tom Clark and David Else. These authors tackle policy issues and federal, state, and local roles related to policymaking and implementation. Their take on emerging issues is particularly interesting in light of more recent essays in Part II. And they give special attention to the leadership role of school principals in the area of distance education policy and practice.

Part II, E-Learning Policy and Practicality Come of Age, is the heart of this volume. The essays in this section are written by individuals who consider various aspects of virtual schooling and e-learning policy. In "Virtual Learning and the Challenge for Public Schools" Barry D. Amis articulates some of the pros and cons of integrating virtual learning into our notions of the common school. Gene I. Maeroff, in his essay, "Motivation and Trust as Foundation Stones of Cyber Learning," raises questions about how students can be motivated to succeed in e-learning environments and suggests that educators "tread on dangerous ground" when they fail to attend to this aspect of effective instruction.

In "Creating a Learning Community in the Virtual Classroom," Nancy M. Davis, who directs the Michigan Virtual High School, discusses the importance of training e-teachers and provides an overview of the MVHS Online Instructor Training course. Texas State Senator Eliot Shapleigh and Chris Cook, in "Improving Equity and Achievement Through Targeted E-Learning Initiatives," discuss government-based initiatives that can boost student achievement across socioeconomic lines of division. Then, in "Virtual Schooling and the Arts: Potential and Limitations," I attempt to delineate the possibilities and the pitfalls inherent in attempting online teaching and learning in subjects that require making, moving, and doing in addition to the cyber-friendly reading, viewing, listening, responding, and writing.

The last two essays in this collection are concerned with Virtual High School Inc. Liz R. Pape, the CEO of VHS Inc., takes the lead with her treatment of "Life in the Cyber Trenches of the Virtual High School." Then, in "Quality Control in Online Schools," Andrew A. Zucker addresses his subject initially in relation to the evaluation of the Virtual High School and goes on to reflect in general about quality control issues related to virtual schools.

An appendix rounds out this volume. Ellen Chamberlain's "Evaluating Website Content" is a useful guide and caution. It is intended not to blunt enthusiasm for e-teaching, e-learning, and online research, but to help users make wise use of Internet resources for educational purposes.

Part I

From Distance Education to Virtual Schooling

Distance Education
and Tomorrow's Schools

Barbara L. Ludlow and Michael C. Duff

Barbara L. Ludlow is a professor of special education at West Virginia University. Michael C. Duff is the owner and media specialist for Discover Video Productions. This essay is excerpted from their Phi Delta Kappa Educational Foundation fastback 439 of the same title, published in 1998.

A simple definition of distance education is any instructional activity in which the instructor and the learner are separated by space or time (Keegan 1988). While the term "distance learning" focuses on the learner's role and the term "distance teaching" emphasizes the instructor's responsibilities, the term "distance education" emphasizes the interactions between the instructor and learner, which are at the heart of education.

Distance education can be as simple as a correspondence course that uses surface mail or as complicated as an interactive television course that combines video, audio, fax, and e-mail. When telecommunications technologies are used for these instructor-learner interactions, the process is known as technology-mediated distance education (Verduin and Clark 1991) because the delivery system filters both content and instruction.

Although early applications of technology for distance education typically used a single delivery mode, newer models employ several technologies to accomplish different goals within the same program. The rapid growth of telecommunications technologies in the last decade and their increasing availability around the globe have stimulated wide-scale expansion in distance education programs.

Trends

Distance education is not a new idea. In the United States it dates from the 1700s, when correspondence courses were offered to train prospective clergymen (Rowntree 1986). Distance education has long been used in remote rural areas in such countries as Australia and Canada. Great Britain established the Open University in 1969 to provide higher education opportunities to nontraditional students, initially using correspondence courses and now moving to telecommunications delivery (Holmberg 1995). And a number of developing countries have used distance education — first correspondence study and more recently satellite broadcasts and Internet connections — to avoid the expense of building schools and colleges (Tiffin and Rajasingham 1995). Several of these countries also are exploring the use of distance education to train professional personnel, including teachers (Perraton 1993).

In the 1980s, telecommunications technology permitted real-time interactions using telephone and television; and educators began to experiment with distance education for high school and college courses and for adult and continuing education workshops (Moore 1991). In 1988 Congress established the Star Schools Program, a federal project to provide funding for educational uses of telecommunications equipment linking colleges and schools (Moore and Kearsley 1996). About the same time, the Annenberg Foundation and the Corporation for Public Broadcasting joined forces to offer funds to colleges and universities to incorporate technology into their delivery systems (Moore and Kearsley 1996).

The continuing development of digital technologies is stimulating the growth of "third generation" delivery systems that combine media to take advantage of their relative strengths (Nipper 1989). The success of these efforts is encouraging more and more educators to consider the possibilities of distance education.

Distance education suits current education theories that focus on learning as a self-directed, active, and collaborative process and view the instructor as a facilitator or guide, rather than a transmitter of knowledge. Distance education provides both instructors and learners with powerful tools for locating, synthesizing, and creating resources in digital "schools without walls." In addition, the current trends in funding public schools and higher education prompt a continual search for more cost-effective delivery systems. Careful selection of available technologies and an appropriate match between media and goals can make distance education the most effective and efficient delivery system for many education programs.

Possibilities and Problems

Distance education presents today's educators with both possibilities and problems. Many educators see distance education as a promising mechanism for improving access to education by increasing the size of service areas (Jacobsen 1994), by reaching nontraditional learners who cannot afford the time and expense associated with on-campus study (Ehrmann 1990), by enhancing the quality of education through multimedia and interactive instruction (Holloway and Ohler 1991), and by controlling costs by increasing enrollments without additional capital investments (Blumenstyk 1994). Emerging technologies offer the hope of establishing an education system that fosters genuine lifelong learning (Halal and Liebowitz 1994).

But distance education is not without its problems. Distance delivery systems can be expensive to develop and operate (Holloway and Ohler 1991). For example, both instructors and learners need special training and ongoing support to use these new technologies effectively, which demands additional personnel resources (Halpern 1994). In addition, some technologies are not available or not as accessible in some geographic areas as in others, and some are too costly or difficult to use for disadvantaged or special needs learners (Kirkup and Jones 1996).

Educators need to weigh these pros and cons before making a decision to use technology-mediated distance education.

Distance Education Technologies

Many different technologies, alone or in combination, have been used successfully to deliver distance education. Some are relatively "low tech," devices that are familiar to most people and require no special training, such as telephones. Others are "high tech," devices that require practice to master, such as compressed video systems. In addition, some technologies (termed "synchronous") allow learning activities to occur as real-time interactions between instructor and learners; other technologies (termed "asynchronous") enable learners to access instructional materials on demand and instructors to respond when needed.

All of the various technologies present opportunities and constraints that educators must understand. At issue is not which technology is better, but how each technology is best used for specific goals.

Low Tech. Two low-tech devices for distance education are correspondence and audioconferencing.

Correspondence courses, which rely on print materials, still are frequently used for adult education and some college degree programs (Rowntree 1986). The print materials may be supplemented by audiotapes or videotapes of recorded lectures or demonstrations to be viewed in conjunction with reading assignments. Learners typically correspond with the instructor by mail, but they also may use the telephone to obtain individualized guidance or feedback.

Correspondence courses are asynchronous. They place no time or place constraints on the learner, and they are relatively low-cost. However, they provide only limited opportunities for interaction with the instructor and rarely any opportunities for interaction with peers.

Audioconferencing has been used to deliver some distance education (Bates 1995). Audioconference instruction typically uses standard telephone equipment (known as "plain old telephone service," or POTS). Any number of learners and instructors in various locations can interact, though a group of people participating at a single site need to use a speaker phone. Instruction is delivered primarily through lectures and discussions, which may be supplemented with print materials. While some audioconferencing systems include fax machines for print materials, most materials must be distributed by the instructor in advance and reviewed by learners before the conference. Assignments and examinations generally are exchanged by mail.

Audioconferencing is a synchronous delivery system that places no constraint on location, but requires learners to interact at a scheduled time. Although numerous sites can be connected simultaneously during a telephone conference, in practice it is difficult to manage interactions among many individuals or large groups who cannot see each other. Lack of face-to-face interaction and limitations on the use of visual media are primary drawbacks.

High Tech. Distance education generally uses one or more of four high-tech systems: broadcast television, compressed video, computer multimedia modules, and online instruction.

Broadcast television delivers distance education by sending analog or digital audio and video signals by microwave relay over short distances or by satellite over longer distances (Zigarell 1991). Microwave systems transmit video signals by means of relay towers stationed at 20-mile intervals, which enables them to cover several hundred square miles. Satellite systems, on the other hand, uplink the signal to one of several satellites and then downlink it to multiple sites within a "footprint" that may cover an entire continent.

Television broadcasts transmit a high-resolution signal that can be used for clear and detailed display of one-way video and audio presentations. Televised instruction often is accompanied by audioconferencing to allow interactions between the instructor and learners before, during, or after instruction. This is a synchronous delivery system that restricts learners to properly equipped places and scheduled times.

Although receiving equipment is inexpensive and widely available, the transmission equipment is expensive and requires specially trained production personnel. A fully equipped studio may cost $100,000 or more. Thus the primary drawback to using broadcast television for distance education is the high development and operational costs.

Compressed video systems employ coaxial or fiber optic telephone lines to transmit two-way audio and video signals for distance education (Duran and Sauer 1997). Compressed video is a synchronous delivery system that restricts learners to properly equipped places and scheduled times. It allows instructors and learners to see and hear each other, but the limited bandwidth for transmission and the effects of compression often result in distorted picture and sound quality.

Compressed video transmission requires a system at each site, which can cost $10,000 to $15,000 each. The originating site also must purchase a code device to encode and decode the video and audio signals and must pay fees to the telephone company for use of one or more special digital IDSN (Integrated Digital Services Network) lines.

Computer multimedia modules are a more sophisticated version of the correspondence course (Kommers, Grabinger, and Dunlap 1996). Instructors package instructional materials, including text, audio, and video, on CD-ROM disks. Learners engage in independent study, but they have only limited contact with the instructor and other learners.

A computer with media capabilities and peripherals, such as a disk recorder and duplicator, are required for developing multimedia materials. The program designer must have considerable expertise in computer programming and the time and energy to produce the modules. And, of course, learners must have access to personal computers with CD-ROM players.

Online instruction uses the Internet and World Wide Web (Kurshan, Harrington, and Milbury 1994). The instructor posts text, audio, and video materials to a site that can be accessed on demand by learners. Sometimes instructors also provide opportunities for interaction through e-mail, listserv discussion groups, or live chat rooms.

Web-based instruction requires knowledge of hypertext markup language (HTML) or a web authoring program. In addition, learners must have access to a computer with either an ethernet connection or a telephone modem and web browser software.

Elementary and Secondary Education

Distance education has been used to enhance public school education at both elementary and secondary levels. Some large-scale applications have been designed by public and private organizations to have national or regional impact, while individual districts, schools, and teachers have developed small-scale applications.

The oldest and simplest application of technology-mediated distance education in the public schools is the use of television broadcasts to facilitate delivery of specialized courses, especially in science, mathematics, and foreign languages. A recent and exciting development is the use of the Internet to involve students from different classrooms in several school districts across state lines or around the world.

Interest currently is growing about the possibility of using compressed video systems to provide consultation with medical and related services specialists to develop and monitor services in the education setting, such as speech and language therapy, occupational or physical therapy, and sign language instruction.

Large-Scale Applications

The Star Schools Project is a federally funded program that was established in the early 1980s to encourage the use of technology in schools through collaborative partnerships between institutions of higher education, state education agencies, local school systems, and businesses. Since 1988 the University of Oklahoma has operated a Star Schools Project to develop, produce, and offer courses taught by college professors in foreign languages, mathematics, and sciences. These courses are available to schools across the country.

The Missouri State School Boards Association maintains a clearinghouse on information about Star Schools Projects (now known collectively as the Education Satellite Network) and operates a Satlink Internet website to provide school systems with information about technology-mediated courses and professional development activities. The Classroom of the Future Project, sponsored by NASA, recently has been active in developing multimedia instructional modules for use by biology students in several states.

Private foundations and corporations also have been active in funding distance education efforts. The TI-IN Network is a corporation located in San Antonio, Texas, that contracts with agencies and individuals to offer elementary and secondary programs and staff development to schools in two dozen states. The company has been active for more than a decade.

Yahoo, a popular online search engine, provides links to websites that offer curriculum resources for families engaged in home schooling. The growth of the home schooling movement has prompted one private consulting firm in California to use online audioconferencing to offer tutorial sessions to students across the country.

State education agencies' interest in distance education has led to the development of statewide education networks, often combining satellite broadcasts, interactive television, and computer networking capabilities. In Virginia, for example, the state satellite system broadcasts content courses in foreign languages, mathematics, and science to schools across the state — sometimes with only one or two learners participating at a given site — with a facilitator at the local school to provide assistance. Hawaii provides access to Advanced Placement courses by using interactive television courses taught by college professors. Indiana has developed a statewide Buddy System to provide computers and modems for families so that students who use the

Internet for learning have access to the same equipment at school and home.

Small-Scale Applications

Some school districts have established their own interactive television systems or computer networks to provide more effective education programs. Larger school districts sometimes have the resources to set up their own technology facilities. In the Toledo Public Schools in Ohio, for example, the International Studies Center uses the World Wide Web for video conferences with students in other countries to promote the learning of foreign languages. The Hillsborough County Public Schools in Tampa, Florida, use a compressed video system to help students with special needs who attend an alternative learning center begin the transition to an inclusive high school by initially participating in high school classes at a distance.

Smaller districts typically need to collaborate with other school systems to take advantage of new technologies. School districts in rural northeastern Utah formed a consortium using television and computers to offer Advanced Placement courses to high school students. A group of school districts in North Florida, with support from community businesses, uses interactive television and video field trips in a conflict resolution program for middle school students. Educators in New Mexico use text telephone devices (TTD) to link hearing-impaired students in different schools in order to develop their oral and written language abilities.

Individual educators also have used Internet and web access to implement distance education for specific groups of students. For example, teachers have used the Florida Information Resource Network (FIRN) to manage collaborative projects in social studies with students in other schools, some in other countries. In Connecticut, special educators have used the Internet to design an electronic penpal program to help students with behavior disorders build social and communication skills.

Implications and Suggestions

Distance education offers hope for solving some of the most pressing problems in education. It can provide elementary and secondary students with access to expert teachers in all content areas, whether the students live in remote rural areas or inner-city environments. It can enable college students to study specialized disciplines through cross-campus distance education agreements. And it can provide accessible, effective preservice and inservice programs. But distance education also presents new problems for educators to solve.

Surprisingly little research has been done to evaluate the outcomes of distance education. Some data suggest that most mechanisms for technology-mediated instruction are as effective as traditional face-to-face instruction (Kozma 1991). Studies also show that while most learners state a clear preference for face-to-face instruction and interpersonal contacts, they generally express satisfaction with distance education because of its greater accessibility (McNabb 1994; Wagner 1993).

Other studies suggest that the most critical feature is learner support through structured instruction, supplemental print materials, and frequent interactions (Dillon 1992; Valcke 1993). Many instructors report that younger learners are less intimidated by technology but may need more assistance in maintaining attention and motivation. On the other hand, they find that more mature learners, initially fearful of technology, are sufficiently experienced to direct their own learning successfully and are highly committed to participating in interactions.

There is some evidence that the relative anonymity and greater time for reflection of asynchronous delivery systems actually may improve participation and increase critical thinking (Burton 1994; Stork and Sproull 1995). On the other hand, the physical and psychological distance created by technology has been shown to decrease the positive affect associated with the learning of content-related values (Culnan and Markus 1987). Some education theorists argue that the type of media used for instruction does not influence learning (Clark 1994), while others assert that media influence not only what people learn but how they learn (Salomon 1997).

Many educators believe that simplistic comparisons between technologies or between traditional and distance delivery are meaningless (Kozma 1994). The Flashlight Project, founded by Annenberg and now operated by the American Association for Higher Education, is developing evaluation tools designed to assist educators in determining the effectiveness, impact, and cost-efficiency of technology-based distance education programs. Future research will need to focus on identifying which education goals can be accomplished best via distance education, as well as which technologies are most efficient in accomplishing specific education outcomes.

Tomorrow's Schools

Distance education has the power to revolutionize education in tomorrow's schools. Technology-mediated distance education creates a vision of schools and universities without walls, freeing learners of all ages from the constraints of time and place and allowing them to learn what they want when they want. Burrus (1993) contends that the necessary technologies already are available, but the challenge is to encourage people to make more effective use of them. And Yates (1995) argues that the most critical goal of education in the next century will be to teach learners how to use technology wisely to solve local and global problems. If society is to realize these visions, educators must learn how to balance equity and excellence by using distance education technologies to enhance access to educational programs and yet ensure high-quality learning experiences.

Two developments in telecommunications technology hold promise for distance education in the future. Scientists are already at work on Internet2, which will provide the high bandwidth needed for real-time, high-speed transmission of video, audio, and data (Van Horn 1998). This development will facilitate the use of desktop videoconferencing and allow immediate online access to audio and video files without downloading them to the desktop.

Second, industry leaders have announced plans to launch a series of low earth-orbit satellites that will allow video, audio, and data to be transmitted around the world on devices similar to cellular telephones (Cook 1997). This development not only will significantly increase bandwidth capacity, but also establish genuinely global connections.

If, or when, these advances become reality, the delivery system will exist to accommodate interactions in real time between any instructor using any medium with any learner in any location throughout the world. Such technologies make possible links between learners and libraries, archives, experts, collaborative learning groups, and special interest discussion groups that will create possibilities for education never before imagined. Educators will come to use these technologies to conduct online personal conferences, to view classrooms for the purpose of preservice instruction, to facilitate peer teacher mentoring and coaching, to participate in cross-cultural discussions of global education issues, and to access resources from a worldwide information network.

The growing presence of distance education at all levels of the education enterprise will result in many important changes. Researchers investigating the role of various telecommunications technologies in promoting acquisition of new knowledge and skills at a distance will offer new insights into the teaching-learning process. Information about the effective use of technology-mediated distance education will lead to modifications in the roles of personnel and the programs that prepare them to work in public schools and institutions of higher education. And, of course, the high initial costs associated with distance education delivery will promote greater collaboration to design and deliver education programs that integrate expertise in subject matter content, instructional design, and production techniques. Technology-mediated distance education represents a vast social experiment; consequently, educators must assume a leadership role in determining how today's technologies will shape tomorrow's schools.

References

Bates, A.W. *Technology, Open Learning, and Distance Education*. New York: Routledge, 1995.

Blumenstyk, G. "Networks to the Rescue? Using Telecommunications Networks to Serve More Students Without the Costs of Building a New Campus." *Chronicle of Higher Education*, 14 December 1994, pp. A21-A22.

Burrus, D. *Technotrends: How to Use Technology to Go Beyond Your Competition*. New York: Harper Business, 1993.

Burton, C. "Using the Internet for Teaching, Learning, and Research." In *Changing College Classrooms: New Teaching and Learning Strategies for an Increasingly Complex World*, edited by D.F. Halpern et al. San Francisco: Jossey-Bass, 1994.

Clark, R.E. "Media Will Never Influence Learning." *Technology Research and Development* 42 (Summer 1994): 21-29.

Cook, W.J. "1997: A New Space Odyssey." *U.S. News and World Report*, 3 March 1997, pp. 55-52.

Culnan, M.J., and Markus, M.L. "Information Technologies." In *Handbook of Organizational Communication*, edited by F.M. Jablin, L.L. Putnam, K.H. Roberts, and L.W. Porter. Newbury Park, Calif.: Sage, 1987.

Dillon, C.L. "Learner Support: The Critical Link in Distance Education." *Distance Education* 13, no. 1 (1992): 29-45.

Duran, J., and Sauer, C. *Mainstream Videoconferencing: A Developer's Guide to Distance Multimedia*. Reading, Mass.: Addison-Wesley, 1997.

Ehrmann, S.C. "Reaching Students, Reaching Resources: Using Technologies to Open the College." *Academic Computing* 4 (April 1990): 10-14, 32-34.

Halal, W.E., and Liebowitz, J. "Telelearning: The Multimedia Revolution." *The Futurist* 28 (November-December 1994): 21-26.

Halpern, D.F. "Rethinking College Instruction in a Changing World." In *Changing College Classrooms: New Teaching and Learning Strategies for an Increasingly Complex World*, edited by D.F. Halpern et al. San Francisco: Jossey-Bass, 1994.

Holloway, R.E., and Ohler, J. "Distance Education in the Next Decade." In *Instructional Technology: Past, Present, and Future*, edited by G.J. Anglin. Englewood, Colo.: Libraries Unlimited, 1991.

Holmberg, B. *Theory and Practice of Distance Education.* 2nd ed. New York: Routledge, 1995.

Jacobson, R.L. "Extending the Reach of 'Virtual' Classrooms." *Chronicle of Higher Education*, 6 July 1994, pp. A19-A21.

Keegan, D. "On Defining Distance Education." In *Distance Education: International Perspectives*, edited by D. Sewart, D. Keegan, and B. Holmberg. New York: Routledge, 1988.

Kirkup, G., and Jones, A. "New Technologies for Open Learning: The Superhighway to the Learning Society?" In *The Learning Society: Challenges and Trends*, edited by P. Raggett, R. Edwards, and N. Small. New York: Routledge, 1996.

Kommers, P.A.M.; Grabinger, S.; and Dunlap, J.C., eds. *Hypermedia Learning Environments: Instructional Design and Integration.* Mahwah, N.J.: Lawrence Erlbaum Associates, 1996.

Kozma, R.B. "Learning with Media." *Review of Educational Research* 61, no. 2 (1991): 172-211.

Kozma, R.B. "Will Media Influence Learning? Reframing the Debate." *Technology Research and Development* 42 (Summer 1994): 7-19.

Kurshan, B.L.; Harrington, M.A.W.; and Milbury, P.G. *An Educator's Guide to Electronic Networking: Creating Virtual Communities.* Syracuse, N.Y.: Syracuse University Press, 1994.

McNabb, J. "Telecourse Effectiveness: Findings in the Current Literature." *Tech Trends* 39, no. 5 (1994): 9-40.

Moore, M.G. "International Aspects of Independent Study." In *The Foundations of American Distance Education*, edited by B.L. Watkins and S.J. Wright. Dubuque, Iowa: Kendall Hunt, 1991.

Moore, M.G., and Kearsley, G. *Distance Education: A Systems View.* Belmont, Calif.: Wadsworth, 1996.

Nipper, S. "Third Generation Distance Learning and Computer Conferencing." In *Mindweave: Communication, Computers, and Distance Education*, edited by R. Mason and A. Kaye. New York: Pergamon, 1989.

Perraton, H., ed. *Distance Education for Teacher Training.* New York: Routledge, 1993.

Rowntree, D. *The Planning and Management of Distance Education.* London: Croom Helm, 1986.

Salomon, G. "Of Mind and Media: How Culture's Symbolic Forms Affect Learning and Thinking." *Phi Delta Kappan* 78 (January 1997): 375-80.

Stork, J., and Sproull, L. "Through a Glass Darkly: What Do People Learn in Videoconferences?" *Human Communication Research* 22, no. 2 (1995): 197-219.

Tiffin, J., and Rajasingham, L. *In Search of the Virtual Class: Education in an Information Society.* New York: Routledge, 1995.

Valcke, M.M.A. "The Actual Use of Embedded Support Devices in Self-Study Materials by Students." *Distance Education* 14, no. 1 (1993): 55-84.

Van Horn, R. "Internet2 and InternetE." *Phi Delta Kappan* 79 (January 1998): 413-14.

Verduin, J.R., and Clark, T.A. *Distance Education: The Foundations of Effective Practice.* San Francisco: Jossey-Bass, 1991.

Wagner, E.D. "Variables Affecting Distance Education Success." *Educational Technology* 33, no. 4 (1993): 28-32.

Yates, B. "The Individual and the Group as Technology-Based Problem Solvers." In *Interactive Learning in the Higher Education Classroom*, edited by H.C. Foyle. Washington, D.C.: National Education Association, 1995.

Zigarell, J. *The Uses of Television in American Higher Education.* New York: Praeger, 1991.

Distance Education, Electronic Networking, and School Policy

Tom Clark and David Else

Tom Clark has been a consultant for education and government enterprises since 1992 as the principal of TA Consulting in Springfield, Illinois. David Else is an associate professor and director of the Institute for Educational Leadership at the University of Northern Iowa in Cedar Falls. This essay is excerpted from their Phi Delta Kappa Educational Foundation fastback 441 of the same title, published in 1998.

Distance education and electronic networking affect school policy at all levels. Educators everywhere are being called on to make and deal with new policies related to the who's, how's, and why's of new electronic communications media. And the policy demands are growing as rapidly as the proliferation of distance education and electronic networking technologies. In Iowa, for example, more than 400 schools will have video and Internet connections through the statewide Iowa Communications Network by the year 2001. Local, regional, and state networks are being created across the country, as schools rush to take advantage of the "information highway."

School administrators have been dealing with distance education policy issues in relation to independent study and satellite courses for many years, but such issues usually have not been central in school policy. Today policy decisions must be made at every level in order for a complete regional or statewide distance education system or electronic network to function effectively. This rapid proliferation is bringing these policy matters to the forefront. And the concepts of distributed learning, learning communities, and virtual schools are creating new policy issues for the future.

In this fastback we focus on policy issues that schools encounter as they become involved with distance education and electronic networking. Our intention is to create a brief resource guide for school administrators, teachers, policy makers, and others interested in policy issues of this sort.

We believe that educators, school board members, and others who shape policy and deal with the consequences of policy need clear information about new distance education and electronic networking issues in order to compete effectively for resources, participate meaningfully in consortia, and competently manage distance education and related technologies in their institutions.

Distance Education and Electronic Networking

Distance education delivery systems are used in a wide range of school activities. We are interested here primarily in those forms of distance education that involve the use of telecommunications, computers, and electronic networking.

Electronic networking refers to the interconnection of computers and other electronic devices in various kinds of networks. Networks can range from the local area networks (LANs) within individual computer labs or administrative offices to campus- or districtwide area networks (WANs), statewide educational telecommunications networks, and the global "network of networks," the Internet.

Electronic networks often are part of distance learning delivery systems. However, their potential use in schools is far broader. Schools are finding that electronic networking can play an important role in technologically integrating the curriculum and meeting education reform goals, as well as in administrative functions, school library information systems, and other areas critical to school effectiveness. We focus on the use of these technologies for learning, rather than for administration.

New Ways of Thinking

Many educators, parents, and students are excited about the new instructional possibilities that can result from the growth in electronic networking. In distributed learning, as envisioned by Dede (1996), "knowledge webs complement teachers, tests, libraries, and archives as sources of information; interactions in virtual communities complement face-to-face relationships in classrooms; and experiences in synthetic environments extend learning-by-doing in real world settings." Whereas classroom-based distance education in many ways replicates traditional classroom teaching across barriers of time and space, distributed learning offers new challenges for education policy makers already dealing with issues arising from "synchronous" methods, such as two-way video. Norris (1997) envisions "knowledge age" learning enterprises transformed by distributed learning.

Another result of electronic networking and distance education is that schools become part of a larger learning community. Networking schools and integrating technology is not sufficient for long-term success. Public schools that join with government and business in local learning communities will stand a much better chance of sustained public support and funding for their networking efforts. They also will keep a larger share of the local education market — not a small concern in a time of high interest in privatization of public education.

Forms of Distance Education

Independent study is the oldest form of distance education and still enrolls more K-12 students than other forms of distance learning. For example, the University of Nebraska-Lincoln's Independent Study High School enrolls nearly 14,000 students annually, more than a third of them in the full diploma program.

A wide variety of media can be used in independent study, including CD-ROMs, videodiscs, videotapes, and audiotapes. The use of electronic networking for communication between teachers and learners is blurring the distinction between independent study and distributed learning. State education agencies usually have a contact person for approval and referral to accredited providers, and some have their own independent study programs. Major providers of K-12 independent study include a number of state universities.

Broadcast and cable television are used by many organizations to provide courses, supplemental and enrichment programming, and staff development. Broadcast television courses, called telecourses, can be viewed live or on videotape by learners in their homes. But most broadcast instructional television programming is noninteractive and intended for videotape use during the school day. Many schools have their own cable-TV community learning systems, used for instructional and interactive programming for students and community members. About three-quarters of all schools have access to cable television, and more than 90% have access to open broadcast programming. Cable TV penetration should grow under the Cable in the Classroom program, especially with availability of telecommunications discounts for schools. Providers include PBS K-12 Learning Services and Cable in the Classroom.

One-way video, two-way audio is live television delivered by satellite or broadcast to schools, with use of the telephone for interaction. A number of organizations offer enrichment, coursework, and staff development by this method. A facilitator or monitor is required, who may be a certified teacher or a classroom aide, depending on state requirements. About one-fifth of schools have access to satellite videoconferencing technology, with higher percentages in rural states. Providers work with specific groups of states, often where their instructors are certified or courses are approved. Major providers include StarNet (previously TI-IN), ASTS, MCET, and SERC.

Video-only satellite is a form used by a number of services to provide supplemental and enrichment programs and staff development. This method uses television programs delivered by satellite without telephone interaction. Channel One, paid for through commercial advertising, reaches some 8 million students through about 12,000 satellite dishes installed in schools nationwide (Levine 1997). Other providers include CNN Newsroom, NASA, NOAA, and SCOLA.

Two-way video, two-way audio is live television with both origination site and participating sites having video origination capabilities, usually along with dedicated audio. Technologies for two-way video include the regular phone line, cable, microwave, and fiber optics, with transmission speeds from a few frames per second through broadcast-quality full motion. States with large-scale, two-way video networks include Iowa, North Carolina, and Georgia. Many hundreds of smaller networks connect schools and districts, with statewide interconnections planned or under way.

Computer-based media are commonly used to supplement conventional instruction. Computer media also have a growing role in independent study and multimedia approaches to distance education. CD-ROM is the fastest growing education technology because it incorporates many multimedia computers and thus decreases software cost. Currently, about 98% of schools own computers, while 85% own multimedia computers. More than half have computers with CD-ROM drives. Use of local area networks (LANs) for sharing computer materials is growing, with about four in 10 schools currently using LANs in instruction.

Computer-mediated communication is used by a number of organizations to offer supplementary instruction, database access, bulletin boards, and discussion groups through dial-up connections. Most of these services are migrating to Web-based interfaces for use by means of local high-speed connections to the Internet. They provide additional sources of information to complement classroom and school libraries.

The Internet is the information highway. For the foreseeable future, the World Wide Web, the Internet's key component, is likely to serve as an umbrella technology uniting distance education media for distributed learning. Applications such as desktop video allow low-cost individual videoconferencing between computers on the Internet. Statewide computer networks with combined audio, video, and data capabilities are replacing earlier dial-up demonstration projects and connecting small regional video networks. Many nonprofit consortia are forming, locally to globally, to use the Internet to provide educational opportunities. National providers include FrEdMail, K12 Net, NASA Spacelink, and World Classroom.

Virtual schooling is the next wave. Some universities now offer complete K-12 courses by "electronic correspondence study," and K-12 "virtual schools" offering complete instructional programs are under development. An example is the University of Nebraska's CLASS (Communication, Learning, Assessment in a Student-centered System), a Web-based course environment. Scheduled for completion in 2001, CLASS will offer an entire high school diploma sequence. Van Horn (1997) suggests a future where students might use "learning pods" distributed among public and private agencies in a larger learning community.

Policy Issues and Roles

A flurry of federal and state legislation, regulation, and direct assistance in the last few years has been aimed at linking schools and libraries to the information highway. The rush to network has created both challenges and opportunities for educators. Following is a summary of the federal, state, and local roles related to policy issues arising from this endeavor.

Federal Role. The general policy role of the federal government has remained unchanged over time, though the emphases have changed under different guiding philosophies. For the most part, federal policy makers are concerned with research, development, dissemination, coordination, advocacy, and legislation. The federal government has only limited direct control over state and local policy. However, federal mandates and incentives can create at least the appearance of reform at the state and local level.

In the last few years, federal policy on distance learning has become focused largely on planning for technology access and integration into the curriculum in support of systemic education reform. We will say more about the evolution of federal initiatives later.

State Role. States are involved in accountability, certification, equity, funding, and quality issues. States mandate standards-based education reforms, often in reaction to standards-based federal initiatives that carry requirements for pass-through funding. They also provide varying amounts of professional development and technical assistance to support these standards and initiatives.

Prior to the growth of distance learning and electronic networking in the 1980s, state policies on school technology were considerably simpler. State education agencies usually had staff for dealing with computers in schools and, later, with technology coordination. With the growth of telecommunications-based distance learning and then the explosion of electronic networking, a number of additional state agencies became involved in distance learning policy.

The role of the state in distance learning and electronic networking can vary from design and implementation of a statewide network with heavy technical assistance to a focus on providing information and resources to support school and district planning. Most states are now addressing equity and access problems through technology, partly through investments in statewide electronic networks and distance learning programs. Some states are providing substantial technical assistance, but most provide only limited funding for staff development, maintenance, upgrades, and technical support. Most states consider these to be district-level responsibilities.

Key state issues for distance learning and electronic networking include system planning, funding, equity and access, and certification. Still on the horizon are such issues as "seat time," which must be addressed if "virtual schooling" approaches are to be mainstreamed.

Local Role. Principals typically exercise management, mediation, and leadership in their schools (Lee, Bryk, and Smith 1993). They coordinate instructional guidance to teachers, establish and enforce building rules and policies, and supervise staff development and evaluation. They also facilitate external communication and communicate about policy decisions internally. Finally, they shape and define formal and informal school goals and provide guidance and supervision in instruction.

It is important for district, regional, and state-level policy makers to take the views of school building administrators into account in reaching distance education policy determinations that will affect the use of communications networks by schools. Local, building-level administrators deal on a day-to-day basis with issues critical to widespread implementation, such as coordination, supervision, and course sharing.

District administrators usually provide facility and strategic planning, administrative direction, and instructional guidance, including staff development, curriculum guidelines and materials, supervision, and assessment. School districts often have moved to meet their instructional needs through distance learning and networking prior to the creation of statewide networks, because they are driven by local situations and circumstances or the need to meet state curriculum mandates.

Local districts (central office) do not figure prominently in contemporary school reform efforts, which are centered at the state level, on one hand, and the local, individual school level, on the other hand (Spillane 1996). However, districts are important in instructional policy because of their major role in providing instructional guidance to schools. In order to support high standards, state-level policy makers strengthen state instructional policies for teachers. This leads to more district-level instructional policy making and often to duplication and unfocused guidance. Some critics would conclude that state-level policy makers should work with districts, rather than ignoring them on these issues.

Emerging Issues

A number of issues are emerging with the proliferation of distance education and electronic networking. Most prominent among them are access and equity.

Thirty-seven of 40 states (92.5%) replying to England's (1991) survey believed that distance education systems can provide a viable alternative for states that must address funding-equity issues among districts. Based on a survey of southeastern states, Jones (1994) found that most were addressing equity and access problems through technology, partly through investments in the statewide electronic networks and distance education programs. However, progress in the development of distance education and electronic networking has been extremely uneven from state to state, related to such factors as rural/urban status, poverty, and ethnicity. Findings about access and equity can be found in the Educational Testing Service report, *Computers and Classrooms* (Coley et al. 1997), which reviewed a number of recent national surveys and studies.

Access to multimedia computers and the Internet in 100% of U.S. classrooms is still a distant goal. About 64% of all public schools have access to the Internet, but only 14% of classrooms have Internet access. Multimedia computer access varies greatly from state to state, with statewide student-to-multimedia computer ratios ranging from 8.5:1 to more than 50:1, with an average of 24:1. The optimal ratio is 5:1.

Universal teacher access to technology training also is a goal. About 20% of teachers used advanced telecommunications in fall 1996. About 13% of teachers took mandated technology training, while 31% received incentives to participate in such training.

Rural schools make more use of advanced telecommunications for distance learning than do other schools (29% as opposed to 22% of all schools), especially satellite-based learning. However, in states without free universal dial-up access for districts, urban school districts are approximately three times more likely than rural school districts to have such access.

Access in high-minority and high-poverty schools is limited. Only 17% of these schools used advanced telecommunications for distance learning. However, with the exception of high-minority schools, poorer schools had better access than wealthier schools to satellite technology. Gains in computing resources achieved in previous years by high-poverty schools through Title I have not continued in this direction.

The National Center for Education Statistics also studied private school technology use in fall 1995 (NCES 1997). Percentages of public and private schools with computers were very similar, but private schools lagged behind in multimedia computers. About one in four private schools had Internet access in fall 1995, compared to 50% of public schools. Only 5% of classrooms in private schools had Internet access, compared to 9% in public schools.

Technology access and use in schools is still far from the "four pillars" goals of universal access to hardware, content, professional development, and connectivity that are essential for technology literacy. The CEO Forum on Education and Technology (1997) estimates that only 3% of schools currently provide a "Target Tech" technology-rich environment needed for true technology literacy. However, the forum also acknowledges that there are no national evaluations under way using tools that actually measure the effects of technology integration on learning progress, quality of content, or levels and kinds of staff development. Evaluating technology integration on a nationwide basis would be a formidable task.

On average, in states surveyed in *The State Networking Report* (Mayer et al. 1997), 50% of K-12 educators and 10% of students were reported to have network access. Yet only 40% of those with network access actually used it. Fully networking schools will have limited usefulness if teachers do not decide to integrate technology into their everyday work. Well-planned professional development opportunities, not mandated use, is key.

Although access and equity are major issues, several other issues are clamoring for attention, including:

Certification. A majority of states require teacher certification for distance instructors. However, it does not appear likely that the use of telecommunications and technology will facilitate a movement toward a national teacher certification program, in spite of some of the advantages that might accrue from such a move.

Scheduling. Among the many challenges associated with distance education is scheduling. Block scheduling stands out as an instructional innovation that may play a role in building the school of the future, which may further challenge distance education. Distance learning that relies on live ("real-time") classroom instruction, whether satellite-based or network-based, generally follows traditional scheduling patterns.

Funding. Finding ways to finance distance education and electronic networking is a major problem for schools. For example, estimates of the cost of putting all U.S. schools and classrooms on the Internet range from $50 billion to $100 billion. The Pelavin Research Institute (1997) offers a wide variety of specific funding strategies for school districts, but it is unlikely that all districts will be able to find a funding strategy that works.

Local control. There is considerable controversy over the effect of federal policy on local control of schools. The Republican congressional leadership has focused on methods of enhancing local control and limiting the influence of the federal government in education reform, has slowed adoption of national testing standards, and has sought to allot education block grants directly to school districts without reporting requirements. State and federal technical assistance may be significantly reduced in this scenario.

School Principals and the Policy Issues

Without the support of superintendents and principals, education reform efforts cannot be implemented successfully. They are key players in technology integration efforts, including those involving large-scale use of distance education. But what about principals in particular?

In 1996 we studied distance education and electronic networking policy issues by surveying Iowa principals whose high schools were connected to the Iowa Communications Network (Clark and Else 1998). An ICN "point of presence" and video classroom site was to be established in at least one high school in each of Iowa's 384 public school districts by June 2000. Internet connectivity using the ICN also was available to institutions obtaining a "point of presence" and video classroom, and most installed such connections. The results of this survey suggest that building administrators whose schools had recently connected with other schools in the region or state through educational networks may face substantial challenges related to coordination and other issues.

Eighty percent or more of principals responding to this survey agreed that the following 10 issues were important for "effective use of the ICN."

1. Teacher/administrator video classroom training.
2. Common semesters.
3. Teacher/administrator Internet training.
4. Matching ICN courses with the best available sites.
5. Common bell schedules.
6. Supervision, proctoring, after-hours staffing.
7. Internet acceptable-use policy.
8. Technical support for hardware, software, network usage.
9. Student Internet training.
10. School/ICN video classroom closings, cancellations.

In addition, the respondents also indicated that most of the policy issues were not being addressed as adequately as they should be. In examining these results, we made several observations in a range of categories:

Coordination. The principals who responded to our survey indicated that coordination with external parties required the most action for networks to be used effectively. Difficulties establishing a common schedule with other schools for ICN video classroom courses were mentioned by many respondents, including several who specifically mentioned difficulties with block scheduling. Substantial numbers mentioned internal scheduling difficulties at their schools related to ICN use and difficulties in sharing course information or coordinating with other schools. Network scheduling also turned out to be more complicated for local decision makers than anyone had anticipated.

Technology training. Clearly, training teachers and administrators to use ICN video classrooms and the Internet were very important issues for respondents, while student Internet training was seen as moderately important. Principals supported staff development for system use early in the process, sharing the sentiment of one respondent that this was crucial to "getting the room used."

Staffing. Issues of staffing and supervision were cited frequently by principals, who often directly or indirectly indicated their own increased time commitment and responsibility. For example, a respondent wrote, "One more responsibility of the principal in a lot of cases — especially when outsiders use the system." Another said, "It does take a lot of someone's time to make sure the building is open and the room is available for installation of equipment, etc."

Facilities and technical support. Some respondents cited construction delays or equipment problems, but most frequently their construction-related responses concerned decisions related to room installation. Some gave highly specific advice for school administrators planning new ICN rooms, such as "placement of room to limit building access for ICN room usage" and "access to restroom during non-school hours."

Leadership issues. Leadership activities to obtain support, such as "visioning" or strategic planning, were named as key issues by a number of respondents. For example, one principal gave as a key issue, "Getting teachers, parents, and students excited about the possibilities. Sharing the vision and having a positive experience right away." Another was more blunt, calling the key issue "'selling' the ICN to instructional staff."

Teacher rewards. Teacher rewards were an important issue for the future, according to the responding principals, though the rewards issue was not as pressing as coordination issues, staffing, or teacher video training. Teacher job security was seen as a "non-issue" by a majority of respondents.

Support for technology use. About 93% of responding principals said their school administration supported the use of distance education, but significantly fewer (72%) agreed that their school's teachers supported distance education. Practically all felt that both teachers and administrators supported Internet use.

Larger and smaller schools. Monk (1986) found that secondary schools with enrollments under 480 had difficulty offering a comprehensive curriculum. We decided that comparing the perceptions of respondents whose high schools had smaller (less than 400 students) and larger (400+) enrollments might yield some interesting results. We found that principals of larger schools rated the importance of student video training less highly than did principals of smaller schools. Principals of smaller schools were less concerned about common bell schedules and semesters than were larger-school principals. Smaller-school principals were more likely to see current access to the Internet and to ICN interactive television courses as adequate and more likely to see staffing for these activities as adequate.

In conclusion, it seems clear that early planning for coordination of courses and curricula needs to be promoted by states through dissemination of models, funding of institutes, providing Internet resources, and other methods. The staffing issues of school administrators also should be addressed, as should rural-urban differences in perceptions. Strategies are needed to promote peer-to-peer networking between schools that use common calendars and schedules and to coordinate courses and curricula between schools with dissimilar calendars or schedules.

References

CEO Forum on Education and Technology. *From Pillars to Progress: Integrating Education & Technology.* Washington, D.C., 1997.

Clark, T.A., and Else, D. "Distance Education Policy and Iowa Schools: A Survey of Administrators." In *Encyclopedia of Distance Educa-*

tion Research in Iowa, Addendum 9-23, 2nd ed. rev. Ames: Iowa Distance Education Alliance, 1998.

Coley, R.J.; Cradler, J.; and Engel, K.P. *Computers and Classrooms: The Status of Technology in U.S. Schools.* Princeton, N.J.: Educational Testing Service, 1997.

Dede, C. "The Evolution of Distance Education." *American Journal of Distance Education* 10, no. 2 (1996): 4-36.

England, R. *A Survey of State-Level Involvement in Distance Education at the Elementary and Secondary Levels.* University Park, Pa.: American Center for the Study of Distance Education, 1991. ERIC Number ED 352 009.

Jones, S. *Educational Technology: K-12 Planning and Investments in the SREB States.* Atlanta: Southern Regional Education Board, 1994. ERIC Number ED 378 947.

Lee, V.E.; Bryk, A.S.; and Smith, J.B. "The Organization of Effective Secondary Schools." In *Review of Research in Education*, edited by L. Darling-Hammond. Washington, D.C.: American Educational Research Association, 1993.

Levine, J. "TV in the Classroom." *Forbes*, 27 January 1997, p. 98.

Mayer, M.; Scarborough, D.; Pollard, J.S.; Stout, C.; and Gamble, C. *The State Networking Report.* Austin: Southwest Educational Development Laboratory and Texas Education Network, 1997. ERIC Number ED 409 003.

Monk, D.H. *Secondary School Enrollment and Curricular Comprehensiveness.* Ithaca, N.Y.: Cornell University, 1986. ERIC Number ED 287 628.

National Center for Education Statistics (NCES). *Advanced Telecommunications in U.S. Private Schools, K-12 Fall 1995.* NCES 97-394. Washington, D.C.: U.S. Department of Education, 1997.

Norris, D.M. *Revolutionary Strategy for the Knowledge Age.* Ann Arbor, Mich.: Society for College and University Planning, 1997.

Pelavin Research Institute. *Investing in School Technology: Strategies to Meet the Funding Challenge.* Washington, D.C.: Office of Educational Technology, U.S. Department of Education, November 1997.

Spillane, J.P. "School District Matter: Local Educational Authorities and State Instructional Policy." *Educational Evaluation and Policy Analysis* 10 (March 1996): 63-87.

Van Horn, Royal. "The Virtual School." *Phi Delta Kappan* 78 (February 1997): 481-82.

Part II

E-Learning Policy and Practicality Come of Age

Virtual Learning and the Challenge for Public Schools

Barry D. Amis

Barry D. Amis has been a teacher in the Philadelphia and Fairfax County, Virginia, schools; a school administrator in Montgomery County, Maryland; an executive with the Association for Supervision and Curriculum Development; and a professor at Michigan State and Purdue universities. Currently he is a writer and consultant in Alexandria, Virginia.

Virtual learning, also called e-learning or Web-based learning, offers unlimited possibilities for redefining how public education is delivered and obtained. It has captured the imagination of a broad array of educators, policy makers, and entrepreneurs. Born out of distance learning and the rapid growth of the Internet, it also is a reflection of the increasing dissatisfaction with the inability of the public school system to meet the needs of all students.

In its 2002 annual 50-state report, "Technology Counts," *Education Week* reported that 12 states have established online programs, five are developing them, 25 permit the establishment of virtual charter schools, and 32 have e-learning initiatives under way. Indeed, *Education Week* said, "cyber schools, online teaching and testing, and other e-learning initiatives are changing how schools operate."[1] WestEd, the Regional Educational Laboratory based in San Francisco, says, "The virtual school movement can be considered the 'next wave' in technology based K-12 education."[2] Finally, in their Call for Action, the congressional Web-Based Education Commission concluded:

> The question is no longer *if* the Internet can be used to transform learning in new and powerful ways. The Commission has found that it can. Nor is the question *should* we invest the time, the energy, and the money necessary to fulfill its promise in defining and shaping new learning opportunity. The Commission believes that we should. The issue before us now is *how* to make good on the Internet's promise for learning.[3]

What is driving this enthusiasm for virtual learning? William J. Bennett, the former Secretary of Education, and David Gelernter have succinctly stated the potential of e-learning:

> [It] can put children in touch with each other and with the world. It can put parents in touch with other parents, with excellent teachers, and with tutors and other consultants. It can create the feel of an actual school with its own school community. It can help motivate, stimulate, entertain, and keep children informed about the world. In sum, it can help deliver a world-class education to virtually any child or adult almost anyplace in the world.[4]

Although the statement reflects overcharged hyperbole, they have described the essential possibilities of virtual learning. Because of these possibilities, Bennett is among those entrepreneurs who have jumped into the realm of virtual learning with the formation of his for-profit online school, K12 Inc., which offers both primary and secondary online education.

Undoubtedly, the possibilities of virtual learning are real and alluring. Yet, as the country moves forward into virtual learning, the challenges for public schools must be considered. Some proponents of virtual learning see it as an alternative to the public school system. If we think of public schools as being operated by publicly elected or appointed school boards that oversee programs and activities and use public funds, then many current ventures or proposals do not meet these criteria. Also, some school officials view virtual learning as a more cost-efficient alternative to building schools. Finally, while there is general agreement that virtual learning can be an effective choice for high school students, there is much discussion about whether it is appropriate for the primary grades. New ventures, such as K12 Inc., are promoting it as a K-12 activity.

Virtual schooling can be a boon to many students by making accessible learning experiences that might not otherwise be available, but there also is the possibility that it can undermine some of the basic tenets and principles of public education. As we move into a new era of electronic and distance learning, we should ensure that the underlying values that have always been a part of American public education are not lost. It is this possibility that I intend to explore so that educators and policy makers will be aware of possible drawbacks to virtual learning as they implement new programs and policies.

In the past decade the list of those who have become disaffected from public schools includes those who have chosen to educate their children at home, advocates for vouchers and tuition tax credits, proponents of charter schools, and some religious conservatives. There also is a constituency that would just as soon privatize public schools and turn them over to for-profit enterprises in the belief that competition and the free market will produce better schools. Virtual schooling is an option around which these various constituencies have begun to coalesce.

Virtual learning is an ideal option for home schooling, given virtual learning's availability at any time and any place. It can provide the resources and support that many parents need to teach their children at home. A natural extension of this type of home schooling is the cyber or virtual charter school. It complements home schooling but allows participants to be part of a larger and supportive community. In those states that support charter schools, virtual charter schools are seeking state funding in the form of vouchers or tuition tax credits. In some communities these virtual charter schools, in one variation or another, are organized and run by for-profit enterprises.

How, then, can virtual learning support the purposes of public education? Ever since the common school movement of the

1830s and 1840s, educating all children in a "common" school-house has been one of the basic tenets of American public education. At that time, according to historian Joel Spring, "It was argued that if children from a variety of religious, social-class, and ethnic backgrounds were educated in common, there would be a decline in hostility and friction among social groups."[5]

This ideal remains as realistic today as it was a century and a half ago. The number of nationalities, ethnic groups, and languages represented by school children today has transformed many of our schools into multicultural centers. Schools across the nation regularly report enrolling students from as many as 30 or 40 countries, and a few see more than that.[6] The diverse backgrounds and rich cultural experiences that these students bring with them make the public schools exemplars of the global society. The learning that results from the interaction among these students is not something that can be transmitted electronically, in spite of the claims of Bennett and Gelernter. That is because children also learn by listening to the voice inflections of their peers, by looking at facial expressions, and by reading body language. The unfortunate incidents of intolerance and harassment that occurred after the September 11 tragedy demonstrate that Americans still need to learn more about one another and the rest of the world.

In his 1916 classic, *Democracy in Education*, John Dewey wrote that participation and social relationships are necessary characteristics of the public school:

> A society which makes provision for participation in its good of all its members on equal terms and which secures flexible readjustment of its institutions through interaction of the different forms of associated life is in so far democratic. Such a society must have a type of education which gives individuals a personal interest in social relationships and control, and the habits of mind which secure social changes without introducing disorder.[7]

We don't want to lose these social relationships and social changes as we move to virtual learning.

The central role that public schools play in American life is seen in the goals of schools and various education organizations. For example, the San Francisco Unified School District Board of Education adopted the following philosophical tenet: "All individuals should learn to live and work in a world that is characterized by interdependence and cultural diversity."[8] The Alliance for Excellent Education says, "A quality education is the building block of good citizenship. . . . these young people will be more capable of being active citizens and participating in the civic life of the nation. In reaching their individual potential, they will also strengthen the social fabric of our society and help overcome the disparities that still divide the American people."[9] The Public Education Network states that "public schools are the critical institutions for breaking the cycle of poverty and redressing social inequities."[10] Historian Patricia Albjerg Graham writes that "academic learning, important as it is, is not the only desirable end of schooling in this society."[11] Although these statements are from very different sources, each affirms that the public school system is much more than just a place for academic training. Indeed, according to the public opinion research organization, Public Agenda, the American people "say schools should not limit education to basics and that high schools should put more emphasis on issues such as drug abuse, tolerance and the environment."[12]

In spite of the opportunities and successes that the public school system has afforded, a persistent inequality, which parallels that of the broader society, has characterized public schools. The common school movement, from which our current public school system grew, was itself controversial. Religious bias, primarily anti-Catholic, characterized the 19th century. There also was the racism and segregation that confronted African Americans and Native Americans. It was not until the *Brown* v. *Board of Education* decision in 1954 that the Supreme Court outlawed the de jure segregation that still existed in 17 Southern and border states. Writing about the ideology and politics of the common school, Joel Spring says that "the protection of a particular set of cultural and religious values was made possible by the way in which control of the school system was organized."[13] It is important to remember this long history of inequality in the public school system because it still influences the attitudes and behaviors of some people today.

The modern public school is much more than just a place to learn the ABCs. The Center on Education Policy has identified fundamental purposes and principles that underlie the U.S. system of public education. These include:

1. Effectively preparing all students for a satisfying life, good job, and active citizenship.
2. Promoting social cohesion and a shared culture.
3. Guaranteeing universal access to a free education.
4. Ensuring equity and non-discrimination.
5. Promoting public accountability and responsiveness.
6. Ensuring religious neutrality while respecting religious freedom.[14]

These principles confirm that, in addition to offering strong academic preparation, the public school system embodies a set of values that the public has deemed important. These values are reflected in activities found in most schools, activities that run the gamut from academic enrichment to sports; orchestral, choral, and drama programs; student government and publications; to a hodgepodge of clubs, intramural activities, and ROTC. In some areas the schools are evolving into community centers with a variety of social services, recreational facilities, meeting rooms, parent centers, and adult learning programs.[15] In many communities the high school, especially with its sports programs, is the hub of community life. Booster clubs, active PTAs, and volunteerism increase parent involvement in the schools. Thus when we talk about the public school, we are talking about a multifaceted entity with a complex array of activities and a broad constituency.

Every period of change in public education has had its attendant controversy. Virtual learning will be no different. There has probably never been a period in the history of the public school when it wasn't subject to fierce criticism because of its perceived shortcomings. Groups that found themselves to be politically, economically, and culturally disadvantaged have recognized public education as a means to improve their status. The advocates for the dominant white, Anglo-American Protestant tradition argue that public education should be organized around the core values of that tradition.[16] Thus the arguments today tend to be about what kind of education should be provided (consider, for example, the often passionate discussions regarding Ebonics, bilingual education, and minority authors) and, increasingly, who should provide that education.

A half-century after *Brown* v. *Board of Education*, we still haven't resolved the issue of equal access to high-quality education, as the debate over school vouchers makes clear. James D. Anderson reminds us that during the school desegregation struggles of the 1950s and 1960s, "the pursuit of academic excellence and the demand for first-rate educational facilities were the underlying causes of the crusade for equal educational opportunity, not the pursuit of liberal social policies for their intrinsic value."[17] This debate about access to high-quality education drives much of the discussion about public schools today. The standards movement is one reflection of that, as are the constant debates over the admissions criteria for selective public schools.

The only democratic response is that every child should have access to a high-quality education. How do we achieve this? Clearly, the public school system has not been able, and is currently unable, to give every student the best possible education.

The disparity in education opportunities has to be addressed and changes must be made if public schools hope to maintain public support. The era of virtual learning offers the possibility of access to high-quality education for all students and may come as close as any system serving a mass audience to offering an individualized learning experience to each student.

The public school system should embrace virtual learning and open itself to new ways of educating students. Many schools have already begun the process. However, public schools should be attentive to a middle-class America that sometimes believes that changes to help underachieving or poor students will come at the expense of their own sons and daughters. When they perceive this danger, they often fight such changes vigorously.

In a discussion of education equity, the Public Education Network comments, "No serious discussion of school reform can progress too far without confronting head-on Americans' feelings and differences about race. Behind conversations about private schools versus public schools, the perceived decline in student achievement or changing admissions policies is an underlying judgment on race and how it affects access to quality education."[18]

In addition, today's media play a much larger role in the public perception of schools. Large-circulation newspapers often have reporters who write exclusively about education. Television provides coverage of high school sports and school legislation, and often there is a dedicated school channel. It is not unusual for political candidates to campaign on an education platform and to receive extensive media coverage for ideas about how to "fix" public schools. The Internet also is a huge resource for information. Most school districts and individual schools have their own websites. Information about school programs, test results, individual school profiles, and much more is available at the click of the mouse. The access to information and the dissemination of information is unlike anything in the past.

But access to information is not the same as access to a good education. The quality of the education that our students receive varies not only from district to district but also from school to school. The blatant racism, class prejudice, and sexism of the past have given way to more subtle forms of unequal treatment, such as the disparity in resources available to inner-city schools compared to their suburban counterparts, the assignment of teachers with the least training and experience to troubled inner-city schools, the use of standardized tests that discriminate against minority students, and the use of admission criteria by selective schools based solely on test scores, which limits the number of students from low-income families who are able to gain admission. Virtual education offers the possibility of overcoming these kinds of problems — if policy makers and educators have the wisdom and the will to use the full potential of Web-based learning.

In spite of general optimism, there are those who see significant obstacles to virtual learning, as two recent commentaries in *Education Week* attest. Among these obstacles, Gwen Solomon and Lynne Schrum say, are the growing standards movement and a consequent emphasis on traditional learning and teaching, a slowdown in the national economy that has reduced the funds available for technology and training, and a traditional inertia that both questions the value of virtual learning and makes pedagogical change difficult.[19] In another commentary, Alan Warhaftig says that "the rush to bring technology to education is motivated more by commerce than evidence of educational value."[20] He adds, "Education is a human enterprise, and while revelations certainly occur while walking on the beach or sitting at a computer, the bulk of academic understanding is best acquired in a classroom — in a community of fellow learners. Students also learn essential life skills in a classroom, including how to interpret meaning — not just in words, but also in voices, eyes, and body language."[21]

The obstacles described by these and other authors may provide a salutary pause to the precipitate rush into virtual learning. Educators and policy makers need some breathing space in order to consider various policy questions, such as:

What effect will virtual learning have on schools? Districts must decide such issues as: whether virtual classes take place in the school or elsewhere; what courses qualify for virtual learning and why, that is, should courses be supplemental or do they include basic offerings; how credit will be allocated; which teachers will participate; what rights to participate in other activities do students have who are enrolled exclusively or primarily in virtual classes; how will attendance be factored into a district's policies; what happens when a student moves to another district or state; how many students in the school can participate; how many students will be in each virtual class; how do you coordinate academic calendars; and what equity issues need to be addressed so that low-income and special needs students are not excluded from participation.

What effect will virtual learning have on students? Some of the issues involving students include: what benefits are lost by not interacting directly with the teacher and other students; is there a minimum technology competency required; will virtual learning be able to accommodate the student's learning style; how will the lack of a formal classroom format affect study habits; will participation in virtual learning mean a loss of participation in other activities; and who do you talk to when things aren't going well. An intriguing issue is how much freedom students will have to facilitate their own education. Will those students who have embraced the use of technology and the Internet be able to redefine current boundaries, or will they have to conform to traditional education practices and restrictions?[22]

What are the cost factors for school systems? Districts need to decide which virtual learning model to choose, for example, state-sanctioned, consortium, or regionally based; college or university-based; virtual charter school; or for-profit providers of curricula, content, and infrastructure. Some districts hope that virtual learning may reduce the need to build new schools and, therefore, save money. This may not be the case. If virtual learning takes place outside the school, who will pay for the purchase and upkeep of equipment? Who will develop new courses and curricula, or will programs have to be purchased from vendors? Will teachers be paid extra for teaching virtual classes? If they teach only virtual classes, to what benefits and privileges will they be entitled?

What about teacher-student interaction and socialization issues? Schools and districts must decide under what conditions it is appropriate for a student to become a full-time virtual learner. The quality of student-teacher interaction and of student-to-student interaction is important. It is equally important that the virtual experience does not create a sense of isolation and, ideally, that it creates a sense of community.

Who certifies the quality of course offerings? One of the big advantages of virtual learning is that it is supposed to make available high-quality learning to all students. If courses are bought from vendors or come from other districts or states, what entity is responsible for certifying the quality? There are regional accrediting agencies that certify regular school programs; and there are specialized agencies, such as the Distance Education and Training Council and the recently established Accreditation Commission for International Internet Education, which may be able to provide appropriate certification for virtual education.

The function of the public school has been vigorously debated from its inception. It has not always opened its doors to everyone; and when it has, its curriculum has been used to support the dominant culture. The common school movement hoped to create a common culture. Ongoing debates about bilingualism and multiculturalism suggest that the creation of a common culture, the old melting-pot concept, is no longer a priority.

Virtual learning offers the possibility to think about schooling, rather than about school. It offers the opportunity to rethink the meaning of basic concepts: school, curriculum, teaching, and learning. Virtual learning offers the possibility of re-examining how public education is delivered and obtained. What can be offered to students no longer needs to be limited by restrictions on access or limitations of space; but first new ideas and programs need to be developed and expanded. Every student can have the opportunity for high-quality education. Virtual learning can become the vehicle for academic learning, and the physical school structure can become the center for other core values and activities.

Notes

1. "Technology Counts 2002," *Education Week*, 9 May 2002, p. 8.

2. Tom Clark, "Virtual Schools: Trends and Issues." *WestEd* (October 2001): 4. www.wested.org/online_pubs/virtualschools.pdf

3. Web-Based Education Commission, "The Power of the Internet for Learning: Moving from Promise to Practice" (December 2000). www.hpcnet.org/cgi-bin/global/a_bus_card.cgi?store_SiteID= 154797

4. William J. Bennett and David Gelernter, "Improving Education With Technology," *Education Week*, 14 March 2001, p. 68.

5. Joel Spring, *The American School: 1642-2000*, 5th ed. (New York: McGraw-Hill, 2001), p. 104.

6. Bailey's Elementary School in the Fairfax County suburbs of Washington, D.C., is typical of these schools. Its students come from more than 40 nations and speak more than 20 languages. The student body is 40% Hispanic, 27% white, 26% Asian, and 7% African American.

7. John Dewey. *Democracy in Education* (New York: Macmillan, 1916). www.ilt.columbia.edu/publications/dewey.html

8. See http://storm.sfusd.edu/

9. Alliance for Excellent Education, *Investing in Excellence: Making Title I Work for All Children* (Washington, D.C., September 2001), p. 26.

10. See www.publiceducation.org

11. Patricia Albjerg Graham, "Delineating the Boundaries of a People's Aspiration," *Education Week*, 27 January 1999, pp. 44-45, 50.

12. See www.publicagenda.org/issues/

13. Spring, *The American School*, p. 129.

14. See the brochure, *Changing Schools, Enduring Principles*, Center on Education Policy, Washington, D.C.

15. The concept of the school serving the entire community is not a new one. In the early 1900s the Gary, Indiana, "schools were open at night and on weekends to serve the entire community." Sheila Curran Bernard and Sarah Mondale, "You Are an American," in *School: The Story of American Public Education*, edited by Sarah Mondale and Sarah B. Patton (Boston: Beacon Press, 2001), p. 91.

16. For example, see Arthur M. Schlesinger Jr., *The Disuniting of America* (Knoxville, Tenn.: Whittle Direct, 1991).

17. James D. Anderson, "Introduction, Part Three: 1950-1980, Separate and Unequal," in *School: The Story of American Public Education*, edited by Mondale and Patton, p. 129.

18. See www.publiceducation.org. For an examination of one school's unsuccessful struggle to maintain diversity when confronted with a hostile middle class, see "Affirmative Reaction," *Education Week*, 6 February 2002, pp. 26-32.

19. Gwen Solomon and Lynne Schrum, "Web-Based Learning: Much to Gain, and Many Barriers," *Education Week*, 26 May 2002, pp. 34-35, 48.

20. Alan Warhaftig, "Web-Based Learning: But the Prom Will Not Be Webcast," *Education Week*, 26 May 2002, pp. 34-35, 48.

21. Ibid.

22. A recent report by the Pew Internet and American Life Project, "The Digital Disconnect: The Widening Gap Between Internet-Savvy Students and Their Schools" (14 August 2002), says in its summary of findings, "Using the Internet is the norm for today's youth." The report goes on to say, "Students are frustrated and increasingly dissatisfied by the digital disconnect they are experiencing at school. They cannot conceive of doing schoolwork without Internet access and yet they are not being given many opportunities in school to take advantage of the Internet." www.pewinternet.org

Motivation and Trust as Foundation Stones of Cyber Learning

Gene I. Maeroff

Gene I. Maeroff is the author of A Classroom of One: How Online Learning Is Changing Our Schools and Colleges, *published in 2003 by Palgrave Macmillan. He is director of the Hechinger Institute on Education and the Media at Teachers College, Columbia University.*

Distance education has always meant delivering learning to students from afar. Correspondence by mail sufficed for generations, eventually supplemented by the technology of the telephone. Instructors and students could hear each other's voices even if they could not see one another. Most of today's cyber learning builds on that relationship and, in some ways, represents an elaboration on the ways of correspondence — providing an ease, speed, and capacity for the written word far exceeding what has been possible by mail. Instructors of online courses say that cyber learning has electronic dialogue at its heart. Thus a key component of the learning flows from the discussions that electronic bulletin boards, chat rooms, and e-mail make possible. However, these communication methods, along with the solitary nature of online courses, also pose special challenges for students and for teachers.

More than classroom-based learning, this kind of education — in which teacher and student are out of each other's sight — revolves around trust and personal responsibility. Furthermore, it does more to place the destiny of students in their own hands, an approach that calls for motivated learners. Admittedly, an irresponsible student may exploit this relationship. Sloth and dishonesty are enemies of online learning. For that matter, though, they are no less unfriendly to in-person education. It is just that everyone is used to some students being lazy and cheating in traditional classrooms.

Bob Weight, who taught at the University of Phoenix Online, trusted his students to assume more responsibility for their education than they would in what he called a "traditional teacher-directed model." In a short paper he distributed to students at the outset of each course, Weight wrote, "We assume that you are motivated to learn, otherwise you wouldn't be here." Given the largely working-adult enrollment in both classroom and online courses at Phoenix, Weight said that he credited students with being "accomplished adults who have achieved some level of success" and told them that he was not about to check up on them.

He wanted them to ask questions electronically of him and of fellow students if they failed to understand something in the course. "I don't track them down or hold their hands," he said in an interview. "I expect them to be responsible adults, just like workers in the real world." He saw his role more as mentor and facilitator than as expert or authority. He strove to establish a peer relationship with members of the class and said that he would "fall all over myself" trying to aid students when they requested help. This trusting attitude translated into flexible deadlines for turning in assignments.

Officials at the Art Institute Online, a for-profit, postsecondary school, said that they found that learners in virtual courses were a self-selected group — self-motivated and typically focused on meeting specific goals and objectives. They said that e-learners value convenience and understand how to use technology as a viable way to learn. "A successful online student has the desire to want to learn and is willing to make the sacrifices of time and effort to do so," a school official said.

Ultimately, in classrooms or online, students generally need to take ever greater responsibility for their learning as they advance beyond the elementary grades. Those fortunate enough to be caught up early in the learning game start motivating themselves more and more, realizing that they cannot count on coddling. They gradually gain a sense of delayed gratification and come to see a connection between what happens in their courses and in their later lives. These students endeavor to complete assignments, turn in homework, and attend class regularly and prepared. Many others, for a whole variety of reasons, do not push themselves and float through school on the raft called social promotion. One might characterize online learning as an experiment in the degree to which students can take ownership over their own education. Like all experiments, it is subject to failure under certain circumstances; and chances for success may be worst with precollegiate youngsters, whose lack of maturity may penalize them in the face of increased independence.

Some institutions try to help students determine if they can exercise the responsibility that distance learning demands. San Diego State University, for example, provides online guidance for students who contemplate enrolling in distance courses, encouraging the sort of self-awareness equally valuable for those who study online and in classrooms — at both the precollegiate and postsecondary levels. A self-administered quiz asks candidates:

- Do I like working and learning on a computer or television?
- Am I comfortable resolving technology problems when they arise?
- Would I want to learn new software or a set of online procedures just to access the course materials or chat with the faculty and others who are taking the course?
- Do I work well alone?
- Am I self-disciplined enough to follow the lessons on my own without peer pressure or pressure from the course instructor?
- Will I be comfortable if I don't get to see the instructor in person?

- Will I be comfortable if I have to ask questions via e-mail? (San Diego State University, "Do I Want to Learn at a Distance Quiz")

Macomb Community College in Warren, Michigan, also offers prospective e-students an online self-assessment, in this case calling for multiple-choice responses to 10 questions. The questions let them gauge their need for the course, their comfort with taking responsibility for learning, whether they could complete tasks on time without reminders, their facility in communicating in writing, their ease in figuring out directions, the importance of feedback from the instructor, whether they found word processing on a home computer easy and fun, their receptiveness to using technology, their facility as readers, and the ease with which they could find a time and place for studying.

Western Governors University (WGU) enables potential students to assess their readiness for cyber learning with a questionnaire asking about their need for face-to-face interaction with instructors and other students, their ability to prioritize tasks, the degree to which classroom discussion helps them, the extent to which they need someone to provide instructions for an assignment, how much feedback they need on their progress, how much desire they have to take distance courses, the time available for such courses, their receptiveness to new software and new technologies, their learning style, and the predictability of their personal and professional schedules.

In helping candidates weigh the appropriateness of online learning, WGU told them that "some distance-delivered classes are even more highly interactive than some classes that occur on campus," "you must be fairly self-directed and conscientious about completing assignments to succeed," you could do well "if classroom discussion is not particularly helpful to you," and that if you are a tactile learner, "it may be somewhat difficult to select distance-delivered classes that will fit your learning preference" (Western Governors University, "Interpretation of Distance Learning Self-Assessment").

The flexibility of online learning is motivation enough for some students. Katrin Tabellion, for instance, found that the

University of Missouri's virtual high school met her needs because her father's job kept the family relocating around the world. "I wanted to get my high school diploma," she said in an interview by e-mail from Ghana, her residence at the time, "but since I was moving quite often, I got the idea of a long-distance course. I just looked up some schools on the Internet and the University of Missouri was most appealing to me. The biggest advantage is that you can choose the time to study or to take your exams. You don't have to be at one place at a certain time. You can do it from anywhere you like." She conceded that despite these incentives, "it is also hard sometimes to make yourself sit down and study. It is easy to say, 'Oh, I'll just wait until tomorrow.'"

What can be done in online programs, though, about students with less motivation than Katrin Tabellion, those who cannot or will not take responsibility for their learning? The formal classroom, in part, is predicated on the assumption that many students lack initiative: Someone needs to prod them. A teacher must watch over them and shield them from distraction. The idea is that sitting in a classroom will block distractions during the time assigned for their learning. Classroom teachers usually take attendance to ensure that students do not cut classes. For the most part, a lack of trust pervades the traditional system. Meanwhile, online learning, with its ability to overcome strictures of time and place, trusts that students will motivate themselves and not take advantage of their freedom. Some call that liberating; others deem it naive.

The system of Carnegie units evolved for secondary school students to provide a kind of guarantee that high schools would expose them to a certain regimen of courses. Carnegie units represent seat time, which cyber learning cannot so easily ensure. The Carnegie unit, which helped put education on a solid footing in the early decades of the 20th century, transformed itself by the final decades of the century into a restraint on teaching and learning. Fealty to seat time can undermine high schools that try to improvise and can hinder the ability of students to take control of their education. The hours devoted to a course assume greater importance than the content of the course. Many schools give little consideration to the fact that some students could complete the course more quickly and that others would gain from having the content stretched over a longer time. The National Association of Secondary School Principals advocated in the 1990s that the Carnegie unit should be redefined or replaced so that high schools no longer equate seat time with learning (NASSP, *Breaking Ranks*).

Education policy makers shun a Pandora's box filled with questions about the nature of the knowledge that students acquire as they amass Carnegie units. A similar situation exists in higher education. It was, in fact, pressure from colleges and universities almost 100 years ago that forced high schools to adopt Carnegie units to make it easier to compare applicants for admission to colleges and universities. Shot through the assumptions is the idea that formal education would hardly occur if students were not in the presence of teachers who deliver course content to them.

Yet the experiences of students who sit in classrooms and nonetheless achieve at low levels demonstrate that such provisions guarantee little about the amount of learning that occurs. Every term in the classrooms of schools and colleges, an appreciable portion of students seems not to comprehend the material, baffled by lessons that teachers offer in the classrooms in which they assemble. The fault may rest with the student, with the teacher, with both, or even with the course material.

Instructors at all levels should recognize the need to motivate students, a task that grows ever more difficult to do without benefit of face-to-face reinforcement. Preparation to teach, in person or online, is incomplete without attention to what teachers can do to prod students to learn. Good teachers take this responsibility to heart and try to draw students into the lessons. Some follow the entertainer route. Some titillate. Some pepper their presentations with nuggets of information designed to make students take notice. Some target individual students, taking a harder stance with those they think need it and softening the approach for those whom they believe require cushioning.

In the hands of a good teacher, motivation is the stealth weapon, designed to sneak up on unsuspecting students, capture them, draw them into the lesson, and impel them to battle with all their fiber to conquer the material. Teachers in elementary schools take this expectation most seriously, and those at colleges and universities feel least responsible for rousing the interest of students in the subject at hand. High school teachers fall somewhere in between in their inclination to engage students. The consumer orientation that ought to be part of the mission of schools and colleges gets short shrift.

Motivation seems linked to maturity, which raises questions about online courses for students below the college level, especially those of elementary school age. At the University of Phoenix, with its working-adult enrollment in both online and classroom-based courses, age and life experience enhance the likelihood of students' maturity. In a presentation at a seminar sponsored by the Hechinger Institute, Craig Swenson, provost and senior vice president for academic affairs at the institution, said that pursuing learning in adulthood leads students to be more self-directed, makes learning more meaningful, and makes learners more effective when their pre-existing competencies are taken into consideration by the instructor.

Maturity provides perspective that may help motivate certain learners at whatever level they study. One of the most responsible students in Ohio's Electronic Classroom of Tomorrow was a woman who had dropped out of a regular high school several years earlier as a pregnant 16-year-old. She never returned to a classroom to complete her studies for a diploma because she had a small child and felt that a traditional school program was not compatible with her lifestyle, not to mention the fact that she would have been older than the other students in the building. She thought that the virtual high school, which she could complete from her home, was a blessing, a chance to obtain a diploma that had more meaning than an equivalency certificate and could open doors to a brighter future for her. She passed all five parts of the state's proficiency test with honors and showed sufficient promise to win a scholarship to Ohio State University.

If their limited life experience raises questions about the motivation of precollegiate students, then it follows that there should be concern about the suitability of online courses for them. A virtual high school in Cincinnati offered a second chance to students who were unsuccessful in traditional schools. However, the cyber school had to drop hundreds of students from its rolls at the end of the 2001-02 school year for what it said was their failure to do the work.

Elsewhere, a revealing study of eighth-grade math students from three ethnically diverse middle schools in two Midwestern school districts identified the key role that teachers play in spurring motivation (Ryan and Patrick 2001). It was important to students' confidence that they perceived their teachers as caring about them and supporting them, attributes that teachers cannot so readily demonstrate online. Another finding in this study, also having apparent implications for online education, dealt even more directly with the connection of interaction to motivation. Students saw instructors as supportive (which, in turn, presumably motivated the students) if instructors promoted interaction and let students collaborate with each other. This finding seems to underscore the value of incorporating online discussion and group assignments into online learning.

Officials at the University of Missouri's virtual high school said that they deliberately tried in their courses to draw out the students, apparently, for the most part, by emulating good classroom practice. The school provided students with learning objectives for each course, a list of assignments, and a study guide that expanded on the lessons and pointed students in profitable directions. Students submitted work online and instructors returned it online, with appropriate comments. "We make it as personal as possible," said Kristi Smalley, principal of the high school.

For many students, the amount and success of the interaction seem to contribute to their satisfaction with the course. It presumably follows that satisfaction leads to motivation. This could be seen in the courses of World Campus of Pennsylvania State University, an entirely online program. Surveyed in the spring of

2001, students in 30 of the courses praised the technology for allowing them "to actively participate in online discussions about the course material," for making it possible "to actively monitor online discussions about the course materials even when I didn't participate," and for supporting "the discussion of ideas and concepts taught in the course with other students." More than 80% of students agreed or strongly agreed with the propositions of the three questions. Seventy percent were satisfied or very satisfied specifically with the interactions with the instructor, and 76.9% felt this way about interactions with other students (World Campus Survey, n.d.).

But interaction, as anyone who has taught will attest, is not easy — even in person. "Few university faculty have the interest or persistence to require every single student in their classes to participate in classroom discussions, much less answer *every* question posed or issue addressed," said Ronald Legon, provost of the University of Baltimore. "The typical situation in the vast majority of classes that even provide the opportunity for meaningful student discussion is that a relative handful of students avail themselves of this opportunity to demonstrate what they know, contribute to the learning process, and hone their speaking skills."

Some students who would be among the silent majority in an actual classroom shine in the virtual classroom, according to Legon. Students who are reticent in the physical presence of the more assertive classmates who dominate discussions may welcome asynchronous interaction. Legon said that asynchronous online discussions, to which students contribute at moments of their own choosing, help them overcome shyness and give students time to mull over responses. Equally important, he added, this approach — allowing the benefit of some extra time — permits those who have lagged in completing an assignment a chance to catch up on the readings. They can weigh in with considered responses when they are ready, instead of trying to bluff their way through, as they might try to do in a classroom in response to questions for which they are unprepared.

Perhaps — admittedly this is a long-shot — online education also suits *some* less obvious candidates, students who have not previously assumed responsibility for their learning in traditional classrooms. This, at least, was the thought in Cincinnati, where the failures of the program do not necessarily mean that the approach could not succeed with better safeguards. Such students might fare better with more latitude for independence if they receive the backup and support that good distance education ought to offer, along with careful monitoring of their progress in online courses.

Motivational research in traditional classrooms shows that to the extent that students choose to perform a task, as opposed to *having* to do it, they are apt to be more motivated. Making more of the decisions about their education may spur some students to learn. E-learning, which offers greater possibilities for empowering learners in this way, could appeal to some students who have enjoyed limited success in classrooms where they chafe under authority.

A fairly substantial body of research underscores the notion of giving students as much discretion for learning as they can handle productively. "Sometimes the students who are disaffected the most from school and would benefit most from practices that enhance motivation are given the least amount of autonomy," wrote Deborah Stipek, dean of the education college at Stanford University and an authority on student motivation (Stipek 1998). Some of her recommendations for providing this autonomy lend themselves to online learning: Allow students to participate in the design of their academic tasks, give students choices in how tasks are completed, let students have some choice in the difficulty levels of assignments or tasks that they complete, and give students some discretion about when they complete particular tasks.

Another factor, peer pressure, prevents some students, especially in secondary schools, from diligently pursuing their studies. They attend schools in which they risk losing social acceptance if their classmates consider them "grinds." These casual attitudes toward academic achievement can foster a milieu unsupportive of hard work. Secondary schools exacerbate the situation when they fail to recognize and reward effort and achievement. Online courses, taken individually, might offer respite from these pressures. In light of past failures, schools need to find something different for alienated students. Maybe virtual learning, properly handled, offers new hope for them.

The experiences of youngsters at the online high school that is part of Daniel Jenkins Academy of Technology in Florida offer a case study of the degree to which students are equipped to accept responsibility. When it admitted its first class in the fall of 2000, the school admitted all 50 applicants without any attempt to sort out those whom the school considered the most promising candidates for e-learning. The district, Polk County Public Schools, had been under court-ordered desegregation for some 30 years and thought it could not screen applicants, as that might smack of racial discrimination. Thus among the 50 entrants were some for whom online learning was unsuitable. Only 34 of the students remained in the school by the end of the academic year, the rest having transferred to the district's traditional high schools.

Principal Sue Braiman said that the school lost students who could not cope with taking six online courses at once. Others just were not accustomed to working without close supervision. "We told them they would have to take responsibility for their own education, and that was a huge leap," Braiman said. "They were used to teachers bringing learning to them." While the high school had none of its own teachers teaching the courses offered by the state at the website, two teachers at Jenkins served as "facilitators," guiding students in setting learning goals for themselves and in managing their use of time.

In 2001, after the high school had existed for a year, almost all of the students completing the middle school level at Jenkins Academy decided to enroll in the virtual high school, which had its headquarters in the building. Students entering ninth grade liked what they had seen and wanted to be part of the grand experiment. The online school, trying not to leave as much to chance as it did the previous year, decided to prepare students for the virtual high school while they were still in the eighth grade. The goal was to equip them to resist the seductions that accompany independent learning, kind of like Odysseus lashing himself to the ship's mast and plugging the ears of the crew to fend off the alluring but dangerous call of the Sirens.

Thus their teachers had encouraged the eighth-graders, one year away from online learning, to handle autonomy. This is no small matter for adolescents, youngsters at an age known for its turbulence. A buddy system paired middle school students with high school students who could share their experiences as virtual learners and show the middle-schoolers the online coursework at the high school level. Teachers at Jenkins encouraged students to set goals and taught them to pace themselves, just as they would have to do once they no longer sat in classrooms with teachers to urge them on in person. "We started weaning them from needing so much help from the teacher," said Braiman. "It was great to see kids make an investment in their learning instead of passively waiting for a teacher to tell them what to do."

Institutions tread on dangerous ground when they offer online courses without regard for the motivation of students. It is fine to place trust in students, but some of them might not be able to handle the freedom. Education online opens doors at all levels to a fresh consideration of how to allocate responsibility for learning. Out of these new ways of looking at motivation may come insights that also will help in dealing with the far larger number of students who pursue their education in classrooms.

References

National Association of Secondary School Principals. *Breaking Ranks: Changing an American Institution*. Reston, Va.: National Association of Secondary School Principals, n.d., pp. 48-49.

Ryan, Allison M., and Patrick, Helen. "The Classroom Social Environment and Changes in Adolescents' Motivation and Engagement During Middle School." *American Educational Research Journal* 38, no. 2 (2001): 437-60.

San Diego State University. "Do I Want to Learn at a Distance?" http://www.distance-educator.com/portals/quiz.html

Stipek, Deborah. *Motivation to Learn: From Theory to Practice*. 3rd ed. Boston: Allyn and Bacon, 1998.

Western Governors University. "Interpretation of Distance Learning Self-Assessment." www.wgu.edu/wgu/self_interpretation.asp

World Campus. "WC Student Surveys: Outcome. Survey—Spring 2001." University Park: Pennsylvania State University, n.d.

Creating a Learning Community in the Virtual Classroom

Nancy M. Davis

Nancy M. Davis is executive director of Michigan Virtual High School in Lansing, Michigan. The Michigan Virtual High School website is www.mivhs.org.

The level of interest in learning online, or "virtual" learning, has grown dramatically during the past five years. Although much of this new growth has been at the college and university level, the K-12 arena, particularly the high school community, has begun to turn attention to this education delivery method as a way to improve student achievement, to increase access in a broad variety of curriculum areas, and to equip students with technology skills.

The first virtual high school in the country was Virtual High School in Concord, Massachusetts, established in 1996 to develop a national model of course development, teacher training, and online high school class offerings. VHS was followed by Florida Virtual High School, now called Florida Virtual School, which focuses on serving home-school students and public and private schools in which curricular needs cannot be met. As the interest grew, Michigan ventured into the mix.

Michigan Enters the Virtual School Movement

Michigan Virtual University (MVU) is a private, nonprofit Michigan corporation, established in 1998 to deliver online education and training opportunities to the Michigan workforce. MVU is a flexible, market-driven organization that contracts for the delivery of its programs and services through Michigan colleges and universities and through private training providers. MVU does not independently grant degrees; instead, credentials are granted by the organization providing the program.

Michigan Virtual University was founded by former Governor John Engler and the Michigan Economic Development Corporation in collaboration with several major industries in the state. The foundation for MVU can be read in Governor Engler's Cyberspeech — "Message on Education and Technology" (4 February 1998, www.michigan.gov).

The MVU prototype was the Michigan Virtual Automotive College, spearheaded in 1996 by the state government, Michigan State University, University of Michigan, and the automotive industry. The automotive college later became a division of MVU and now has an expanded focus as the Michigan Manufacturing Training Network.

MVU is governed by a board of directors composed of representatives of the state's employer and education communities and state government. The MVU board currently includes the state superintendent of public instruction and the executive director of the Michigan Education Association, the largest teachers union in the state.

The Michigan Virtual High School was approved by the legislature in June 2000. It was funded for three years to gain an initial toehold in the K-12 arena and to advance the use of technology as an instructional delivery mechanism for secondary schools. The purpose of MVHS is to enhance and supplement the school curriculum and to provide online tools and resources to students, educators, and parents. In just two years, MVHS has become a resource to more than 210 public and nonpublic high schools (out of 1,100), serving more than 5,000 students with online courses. The course subjects draw from Advanced Placement, core curriculum, and electives. MVHS also offers a variety of online test tools, licensing content from Apex Learning, class.com, and TestU, as well as developing high school courses and state assessment tools specifically for the Michigan school population to meet the state curriculum frameworks and standards.

Training Online Instructors

Teachers from across Michigan are invited to apply for the Online Instructor Training course. Applicants' areas of certification, credentials, and technology expertise are reviewed prior to acceptance. An MVHS goal is to train one teacher from every high school in the state as a way to infuse the entire state system with a thorough understanding of how online learning fits within the curriculum of Michigan's secondary schools.

MVHS does not grant degrees, issue diplomas, or directly grant credit. Instead, courses and resources are offered to schools through a partnership arrangement (now known as the MVHS Subscription Model). Schools control the classroom conditions, including such variables as credit, grade reports, and transcripts.

Because of the MVHS role of "complementing, not competing" with schools, teachers are a key to the success of both course development and online teaching and learning. Thus a major feature of MVHS has been its focus on training secondary teachers to understand and integrate online learning into their curricula.

When MVHS began, there were many questions and concerns about the effect that virtual learning would have on established schools. For example, many teachers believed that virtual classes would eliminate teachers' jobs. However, online learning does not eliminate jobs; it changes some jobs once it is embraced in schools. To help allay these concerns, Michigan's two teacher unions, the Michigan Education Association and the Michigan Federation of Teachers, were invited to participate in an MVHS advisory group.

MVHS reviewed existing training models in the area of online teaching and found that most of them were geared to college learning environments. The modules did not have the structure and discipline needed to train teachers to handle adolescents in the virtual classroom. Consequently, MVHS designed its own MVHS Online Instructor Training Program (commonly referred to as the MVHS OIT course), which has now trained more than 175 Michigan educators to teach classes offered through MVHS.

In the first year school partners were given guidance on establishing a policy to govern the application of virtual classes within the school district curriculum. The Michigan Department of Education also established guidelines for virtual classes that govern the relationship of virtual classes and pupil funding levels. Currently high schools may allow students to take two virtual classes per semester and, if coupled with additional "in seat" courses, to collect the full-time equivalent rate per student.

The bases for the online instructor training course are the concepts of sound teaching and learning and classroom management. The OIT course introduces potential MVHS instructors to the online teaching environment and to theories and techniques for effectively teaching and learning online. These include establishing professional relationships among interested Michigan educators so that they have help and companionship. The course emphasizes the formation of a learning community and provides modeling and specific practice in managing a virtual classroom.

The MVHS OIT course uses Blackboard, whose makers describe it as an "e-education suite of enterprise software," as a course-hosting environment. Thus most of the skill development is focused on successfully learning how to navigate in this environment. Equally important are coaching and support aimed at developing positive attitudes about online learning, creating a positive tone and climate for the online classroom, and establishing friendly but professional relationships with high school students online. Resource development includes both interaction with peers, who become resources to one another as they teach, and identification of online resources and tools that are available to online instructors and are current and relevant to the field.

OIT Course Components

The OIT course begins with one full day of face-to-face training at the Michigan Virtual University offices in Lansing. Using
the Global Collaboration Center — a high-tech facility with
video teleconferencing, 24 laptops, Internet access, a smart
board, and video projection — teachers are first immersed in the
world of MVHS and its purpose and mission. Prior to the first
session, teachers are given an assignment that gives them initial
familiarity with the classroom structure; and they post information on their personal information page.

After the full day of onsite training, the rest of the OIT course
is online. Through a series of modules, interactive sessions, group
assignments, and individual work, teachers are given the experience of being a student in an online course while they are being
taught the pedagogy of online instruction. This portion of the
course lasts six or seven weeks, depending on the time of year
(factoring in holidays), and it requires teachers to be online about
five to seven hours each week.

The course is divided into the following topic areas:

- Understanding the Virtual Learning Environment
- Becoming a Virtual Learning Community
- Developing Virtual Relationships
- Managing the Virtual Learning Environment
- Designing the Virtual Learning Environment

There are fundamental differences between being an effective
traditional classroom teacher and an effective online teacher. In
the MVHS training, teachers learn how to transfer the best skills
of traditional classroom teaching to the virtual classroom environment. Teachers learn methods for developing positive relationships that will ensure their success as an online teacher for
MVHS. The course also is intended to model methods that will
be useful to these teachers once they take an assignment to teach
online. As important as learning these skills is the creation of a
learning community that establishes a network of support from
peers in the MVHS online world.

Responses to the Training

This course has been offered every three to four months and continues to be rated very highly by the participants. In evaluation data collected by MVHS, levels of difficulty are assessed on the content, as well as attitudinal data from the instructors about their course experience. Overwhelmingly, teachers view this experience as one of the "best professional development" experiences they have had.

Among the 175 teachers trained to date, there is an almost equal split between seasoned veteran teachers with more than 20 years of classroom experience and those with less than 10 years. This blending of new and older teachers works very well; many of the younger teachers are better versed in technology tools, and the older group has a wealth of experience to share.

The first module, Understanding the Virtual Learning Environment, is rated as the "easiest"; the fourth module, Managing the Virtual Learning Environment, is the most difficult. In the latter module, teachers learn that the tools of the virtual classroom (using the digital drop box, discussion boards, chat rooms, group communication tools, and so on) can become overwhelming if not well monitored. One session, for example, pushes teachers to learn from experience about "quality versus quantity." They soon discover that "quantity" is not necessarily a good thing in the virtual classroom.

Many of the newly trained "cyber-pioneers" summarize their experience as this individual did:

> Sharing ideas with professionals that had a desire to learn and expand their vision was extremely satisfying. Often in face-to-face (traditional) training, we spend too much time grousing about things that are weighing us down instead of working towards a better future. I think all teachers should have some sort of discussion board.

Another participant stated:

> I learned that my fellow teachers are just as interested as I am in the issues surrounding online education.

And finally:

> There is no way to hide in the virtual classroom. Every member of the learning community must participate, and this is done in a very nonjudgmental way. If only all of our classrooms could be as democratic.

In addition, such important areas as time management, dealing with the unruly student and disciplinary actions, and proper communication techniques are all found to be extremely important to the online teacher trainees. They finish the course but continue to be members of the MVHS "Instructor's Corner," which becomes the equivalent of a school faculty lounge and allows MVHS staff to communicate regularly with the trained teachers.

During a recent semester, 50 of the MVHS-trained teachers delivered instruction to Michigan students through the Michigan Virtual High School. The continued success of our OIT course will ensure that these professionals have a solid learning community, brought to them anytime, anywhere, through the tools of technology and the Internet.

Improving Equity and Achievement Through Targeted E-Learning Initiatives

Eliot Shapleigh and Chris Cook

Eliot Shapleigh is a Democratic state senator in Texas representing District 29 in the El Paso area. He is a graduate of Rice University and holds a law degree from the University of Texas School of Law. Chris Cook serves as Senator Shapleigh's chief of staff and holds a Master of Social Work degree from the University of Michigan.

One of our nation's most important goals is the production of more college graduates. Persons with college degrees have significantly higher incomes and make greater contributions to the economy. Yet some states, such as Texas, are facing declining college enrollment. And while some states have set ambitious goals for increasing the number of students entering higher education, these goals will not be achieved without dramatically changing the way education services are delivered.

The nation already experiences significant gaps among geographic, racial, and ethnic groups in academic performance, college enrollment, and graduation, as well as access to education resources. Such factors as poverty, level of parents' education, a student's cultural environment, and prejudice and discrimination also influence achievement and therefore the likelihood of college enrollment. Statistics show higher numbers of minority students are channeled into disciplinary alternative programs in which learning opportunities are severely limited.

Contending with academic failures also is costly. About half of students who repeat a grade do no better the second time, and such retention is believed to cost the country an average of $10 billion per year. Channeling these resources into efforts that will improve performance should prove a more prudent use of funds.

The magnitude of traditionally higher dropout rates and lower levels of educational attainment among minority populations will increase if current patterns and practices continue, given the projected growth in the Hispanic population. African Americans, Latinos, and Native Americans make up one-third of the U.S. population under age 18 and by 2030 will constitute two-fifths of the population (College Board 1999).

In some parts of Texas, for example, as much as one-third of the state's adult population has less than a ninth-grade education (Murdock 2002). Latino children are more likely to leave school early, and most of those who leave do so by the ninth grade (Tornatzky et al. 2002). In the United States, 36.5% of white high school graduates ages 25 to 29 had earned at least a bachelor's degree by 2001, compared to 20.6% of blacks and 16.4% of Hispanics, according to the U.S. Census.

In the face of such statistics, educators are looking to e-learning strategies as a means of achieving academic goals that lead to increased higher education enrollment. In this essay we urge the identification of barriers to education, from preschool through college, with an eye toward an array of interventions, including e-learning, to improve education outcomes. Key to the proposed strategies is recognition that e-learning should be but one intervention along with other community-supported activities that are aimed at reducing the social and economic barriers to academic success.

We discuss a few of the profound gaps in education access and performance and the e-learning strategies that can help to close them. However, the mere availability of computer-based classes and materials will not guarantee dramatic academic improvement. In fact, until individual students have their own laptop computers and electronic learning materials are widespread and accessible for every learning need, schools will need to target their use strategically in order to fill the greatest gaps or to make the most difference to achieve measurable education outcomes. Furthermore, teachers will need access to electronic tools that reduce the time they spend in administrative tasks so that they can direct more attention to assessing and then improving student performance.

States and the federal government must examine the extent to which current funding, administrative requirements, and education policies may be impeding the use of e-learning. By systematically assessing performance and learning needs at the district, school, classroom, and individual student levels and by bringing the right tools to the age and grade levels where a student may most benefit from them, the country can make higher education and its associated benefits a reality for a dramatically larger group of people.

Studies show that technology can enhance education outcomes, especially if its use is tied to school reform and integrated into instructional delivery. Effective strategies will call for state and local education leaders to work with community partners to target the right e-learning tools (such as online courses) where they are most needed and to augment those tools with other technological and non-technological supports.

Following a discussion of challenging barriers to progress along the education pipeline and available e-learning solutions, we propose a process that can be adopted at the macro (state or school district) or micro (classroom or individual student) level for targeting limited e-learning resources where they can make the most difference in achieving academic success. We conclude by discussing legislative initiatives that can expand e-learning, thereby making a difference in education outcomes.

Gaps in Access and Performance: The Education Pipeline Concept

Educators universally accept that children's academic achievement is contingent on their mastery of critical skills and attainment of knowledge at each stage of development. At each age and grade along the education pipeline, from preschool to high school, barriers to mastery exist; and interventions for removing or mitigating the barriers are possible.

Major gateways exist for academic success: language acquisition, reading mastery, and math proficiency (particularly algebra). E-learning can break down barriers in the pipeline and address gaps in access to resources that can impede students' progress as they move through the education pipeline.

Language Acquisition and Reading. Research shows the benefits of a prekindergarten education, including higher high school graduation rates, lower unemployment rates, higher scores on standardized tests, less need for remediation, and better school attendance by children who start well, as compared to children who do not participate in early childhood education. Success is attributed to the skills that the children gain in verbal achievement, perceptual reasoning, and social competence. Yet only 20% of Latino children under age 5 are enrolled in early childhood education, compared to 44% of African Americans and 42% of whites (Tornatzky et al. 2002).

Because language acquisition is a primary developmental task from infancy through preschool, policy makers must consider the resources, such as Head Start programs, needed to foster this critical skill. Funding such programs is critical to ensure widespread academic achievement. Until such funding is adequate to provide programs on a widespread basis, educators must seek ways to improve language acquisition as early as possible.

Children who demonstrate language deficits could use age-appropriate electronic applications that "listen" to the student's use and pronunciation of words, identify deficits, and then customize exercises based on the specific aspect of language that needs to be mastered. Such applications can provide the user with thousands of repetitions specifically where learning is needed, while bypassing material that already has been mastered. Early learning programs involving age-specific computer software can help preschool children meet early learning goals.

Language acquisition is even more complex for students who do not speak English as a primary language in the home. More than 3.4 million students were limited in English proficiency in 1998, up 48% since 1995 with another one million projected to enroll in schools by 2003, according to the National Clearinghouse for Bilingual Education. Persons with limited English proficiency have much lower rates of academic achievement by a variety of measures, in part because of limited exposure to the language. Using e-learning resources to increase time spent on learning and exposure to English as early as possible will yield outcomes that otherwise are not likely to be achieved.

Mathematics Proficiency. One of the most significant areas in which e-learning could make a difference in academic performance is mathematics. Algebra, in particular, was designated as a "gatekeeper" course by the College Board after a 1993 study revealed that successful completion of high school algebra or geometry is a major indicator of successful entrance into college. In fact, for students who completed high school geometry, 83% of white students and 80% of African-American students enrolled in college. Given this connection, it makes sense to target e-learning resources in this direction. Academic performance gaps in this area underscore the need to do so. In Texas, for example, the end-of-course pass rates for Algebra I were at 51% in 2001. In three Texas border school districts — Anthony, Canutillo, and Fabens — the pass rates that year were 5%, 20%, and 21% respectively.

The use of tutorials, online supplemental courses, or other e-learning tools in algebra could significantly change dismal performance rankings. One successful program designed for in-school use is Project SEED, which is supported by mathematicians, engineers, and scientists. This program could be adapted as a supplemental program and incorporate e-learning (College Board 1999). The best electronic math tools are those that can identify an individual student's current level of understanding, begin at that level of understanding, and provide enough progressively challenging learning repetitions to ensure that the student grasps a concept before moving on.

Access to Technology. One barrier to achieving equity in education is known as the *digital divide*, or the gap between those who have access to computer equipment and those who do not. This physical access issue can be examined in terms of the number of computers per student in a classroom, the percentage of students who have access to a computer at home, and the capacity of the available technology, for example, access to high-speed Internet connections. However they are measured, gaps are noted between wealthy and poor districts, among households, and among racial groups. For example, households with a per capita income of more than $75,000 are more likely to have Internet access at home; non-Hispanic white households are more likely to have Internet access; and wealthier school districts are more likely to have Internet connections in classrooms. Teachers are more likely to use computers or the Internet in low-minority and low-poverty schools (57%) than in high-minority and high-poverty schools (Tornatzky et al. 2002).

Whatever these physical access issues may be, education policy experts also emphasize the futility of filling gaps by providing equipment without also providing for its strategic use to achieve outcomes. This entails ensuring that the school has the ability to maintain the equipment and support its users and that teachers have been provided training to use the equipment to achieve learning objectives.

State and federal policies have attempted, with some success, to mitigate physical access gaps by funding hardware, software, and connectivity in schools. Discrepancies still exist, however.

Technology innovators contend that the way to alter learning dramatically is to put the technology in the hands of the learner and to immerse entire schools in technology use. However, mere distribution of equipment does not ensure successful outcomes. In the future, more attention must be paid to the optimal use of equipment and the measurement of results.

Access to Certified Teachers or Tutorial Support. One type of education inequity occurs when a student cannot take a course because a teacher is not available or when a course must be taught by a teacher not certified in the subject. Furthermore, some students do not have access to teaching supports that might help them excel academically in challenging subjects. Some equity issues associated with the need for access to teachers or tutoring, which might be mitigated or solved by technology, include:

- Girls may be less prepared than boys in certain school subjects, while boys lag behind girls in others.
- Rural schools may find it difficult to hire teachers in certain subjects.
- Completion of rigorous coursework is a significant factor in graduation from college, yet as many as 100,000 capable students nationwide may be denied access to Advanced Placement classes (Gira 2002, p. 5).
- Special education students may experience dysgraphia that prevents legible writing.

A Strategy for Closing the Gaps

A holistic approach to improving education outcomes is needed. The approach should incorporate individualized strategies, including e-learning. This type of approach recognizes that merely linking a student to a course on a computer will not necessarily yield positive results. Studies involving the use of online learning suggest that other actions often must accompany computer availability or an online course. Such actions include, for example, training teachers so that they can best use the equipment and support a student's e-learning.

Individualized education has not been seen as universally practical because of the amount of support required. Teacher time spent in administrative tasks — such as paperwork, assignment and test grading, and the like — must be reduced to allow increased attention to planning and directing individualized learning. In an optimal learning environment, teachers would have access to automated tests and interactive teaching tools that reduce preparation time and free up targeted teaching time.

This holistic strategy for achieving academic success involves four phases, and technology — especially e-learning — has a role in each of these phases:

1. Assessment. A district generates critical data on its demographics, risk factors, and academic performance at the district, school, classroom, and individual student level. Districts can profile themselves relative to other districts in the state and identify performance or achievement gaps at the classroom and student level. Some indicators of equity and access that provide districts with information from which to build academic improvement strategies include:

- Funding per pupil.
- Dropout rates.
- Subject pass rates (for example, in algebra) by district.
- Number of students who do not use English as a primary language at home.
- Percentage of a school's graduates enrolled in college-prep or AP courses; percentage of graduates taking AP tests.
- Attendance.
- Per capita income in the area.
- Immigrant status and nativity.
- Percentage of teachers not certified in the courses they teach.
- Individual students' scores on achievement tests, grades, etc., for several years.
- Percentage of students on a rigorous college preparatory track.
- Grade-level pass rates and high school graduation rates.
- Student-to-computer ratio.
- Teacher receptivity and preparation to implement technology.
- Socioeconomic indicators, such as unemployment, per capita income, and housing.
- Number of ninth-grade second- and third-year freshmen.

- Percentage of children placed in disciplinary alternative programs.
- Percentage of students who enter ninth grade and complete high school within four years.

A significant amount of assessment information usually can be obtained at the district level. Arizona and Massachusetts, for example, both have education portals with unique sign-on clearances for teachers and students. The ability to generate assessment data in real time makes this strategy even more viable.

Another example: The Texas Business and Education Coalition has devised the PIPE (Performance Information for Public Education) program for its state and has piloted the program in five school districts.* Depending on clearance levels, the system generates such information as student performance at the district, classroom, and individual student level. One valuable facet of this program is the ability to look at a student's progress over time even if he or she attended different school districts in the state, thereby eliminating some of the discontinuity that occurs for children who must move frequently. More than 1,000 school districts could voluntarily become part of this system for about $16 million, plus ongoing maintenance costs. Similar tools also are being developed by state education agencies.

2. Strategy Development. This phase involves examining the assessment data, identifying areas where interventions are possible, and figuring out how to direct resources to where they are needed. This phase could be completed in an inclusive manner with the participation of private-sector community leaders, educators, social service providers, parents, and others. At the close of this phase, the participants will have identified the e-learning solutions that are likely to have a positive effect on academic achievement, along with any accompanying needed social, monetary, or education support.

---

*For more information, see the Texas Business and Education Coalition website at http://www.tbec.org or the PIPE website at http://pipe.triand.com.

Some states are facilitating local strategy development through the establishment of Web-based education portals that help teachers, students, and parents find approved e-learning tools to meet specific education needs. For example, Arizona procured and delivered free of charge an array of software titles to schools through the Internet, along with Web-based administrative tools, such as e-mail, grading and testing tools, and teacher websites. When actual educational materials or information about such materials are offered through a portal, schools can realize considerable cost savings.

Communities that foster relationships with companies that have expertise in education technology will have access to additional solutions. The Intel Model School Program, for example, provides grants to schools that need technology.

A successful strategy for many students is increased use of supplementary education opportunities. Such programs typically operate outside normal school hours. With e-learning, opportunities to make good use of these hours could be expanded to include hours when students are at home.

3. Implementation. Identified solutions are carried out. At this point, the resources needed are obtained, distributed, and put to use. One significant role a state agency can play in this phase is to offer selected districts or classrooms scholarships for "seats" for online courses they deem necessary to fill equity gaps or to help students reach academic goals. States can work on ensuring that resources are available to fill documented gaps. Under this strategy, districts would submit requests for e-learning equity funding, and the state agency would allocate resources where they will have the greatest effect on academic success.

4. Evaluation. In this phase, the effects of the intervention are quantified and reported.

Two primary impediments to implementing this holistic approach are funding and the investment of teachers' time in planning and administering individualized student plans. Although a variety of funding sources exist, schools could benefit from help in identifying these sources. Community teams also can be instrumental in generating private-sector support once customized local strategies are developed. Title I of the federal Elementary and Secondary Education Act of 1965 offers funding that is specifically aimed at improving the academic achievement of the disadvantaged. This act has been criticized as ineffective because funds were directed largely at salaries for Title I administrators, aides, and teacher assistants. Its creative use for e-learning solutions, especially to improve early reading acquisition, should be explored diligently. The U.S. Department of Education also offers grants to provide low-income students access to Advanced Placement courses over the Internet and to pay AP exam fees.

Other Policy Strategies

Recent research shows that the digital divide is closing. However, few schools can boast that each child has access to a handheld computer to carry to and from school and from one classroom to the next. Seeking ways to obtain such equipment is a worthwhile goal, as long as strategies for computer use also are developed.

Technology Immersion. One strategy for making equipment available was adopted by the Texas Legislature in June 2001 as S.B. 1458, 77th Legislature. This bill allows school districts in Texas to accept used computers from state agencies and private donors and to pass along the equipment to students who would not otherwise have access to computers at home. Recipient school districts exercise local discretion in refurbishing the used computers or in passing them along in their existing condition. Rules for implementing the transfer of equipment also depend on local discretion, except that school districts must give preference to educationally disadvantaged students without home computers. The state also relies on its Texas Infrastructure Fund to fund initiatives to expand technology access.

Technology immersion goes beyond making equipment available to students, however. In a true "school of the future," conable to students, however. In a true "school of the future," conventional ideas about the way teachers teach, children learn, schools are built, classrooms are arranged, school schedules are set, and buildings constructed will all be challenged. Classrooms set up as "pods," in which students can collaborate or seek teacher consultation and then return to individual stations, are a promising alternative to the traditional classroom organization.

In the 78th Legislative Session, lawmakers will consider opportunities to test the benefits of technology immersion in selected schools. Funding to implement such demonstrations in these tight budget times will challenge the initiatives, but the selective targeting of funds where equity or performance gaps exist should be viewed as a more cost-effective approach than blanket funding for school districts. In the long run, these technology solutions will save in infrastructure costs and help educators reduce the amount of time spent on administrative duties, thereby increasing time spent in value-added activities with students.

Ensure Funding Flexibility for E-Learning Materials. States should examine current funding formulas and rules to ensure that districts may purchase e-learning materials with at least as much flexibility as they may currently choose textbooks. In Texas, districts may select textbooks from a list of state-approved sources using an established funding allocation. By making it clear in state law that districts may designate any portion of their textbook allocation for the purchase of electronic learning materials, districts can expand the use of such materials.

The benefits of such a strategy may be relatively small as long as each student does not have a computer. Until each student has electronic access to texts at home *and* in the classroom, a significant shift away from the costly paper texts may be unlikely. But this reality does not eliminate the need for administrators and policy makers to work with textbook companies to modernize the use of text-based materials for learning.

Conclusion

Changing demographics and current academic performance

ratings present serious challenges to educators and policy makers. If the United States continues with its traditional methods of delivering education to students, then its academic performance inevitably will worsen. Research already has documented the differences across the nation in access to education resources. Securing funding to equalize these differences through traditional delivery methods would be daunting, if not impossible. E-learning, especially when delivered in conjunction with services that mitigate the other impediments to learning — such as poverty — offers a cost-effective alternative for filling gaps in access and performance.

A case can easily be made for using technology to conduct more detailed assessments on several levels in the education system, including district, school, classroom, and student levels. The case is further made for finding ways to shift the percentage of teacher and administrator time away from administrative tasks, such as grading papers, toward individualized student planning and teaching. This shift can be realized through the adoption of electronic teaching, testing, and grading tools that do the work for the instructors. With teacher time freed up, it becomes more feasible to examine individual student performance — and to find and deliver resources to help individual students.

References

College Board. *Reaching the Top: A Report of the National Task Force on Minority High Achievement.* New York, 1999.

Gira, Rob. "Jay Mathews: Continuing the Class Struggle for Access to Rigorous Courses." *ACCESS: AVID's Research Journal* 8 (Winter 2002). www.avidonline.org

Murdock, Steve. *The Population of Texas: Historical Patterns and Future Trends Affecting Education.* Testimony before the Texas Senate Business and Commerce Committee, Subcommittee on Interim Charge #4, 9 January 2002.

Tornatzky, Louis G.; Macias, Elsa E.; and Jones, Sara. "Latinos and Information Technology: The Promise and the Challenge." Claremont, Calif.: Tomás Rivera Policy Institute, February 2002. www.trpi.org/

Virtual Schooling and the Arts: Potential and Limitations

Donovan R. Walling

Donovan R. Walling is the author of Rethinking How Art Is Taught: A Critical Convergence, *published in 2000 by Corwin Press. He is director of publications and research at Phi Delta Kappa International.*

In a world that views things "virtual" (e-commerce, cybercash, digital networks) as commonplace, it is useful to recall that *virtual* once meant — and still means — "existing in essence, not in fact." In a word, *simulated*. Is virtual schooling a form of simulated education, rather than real education? The answer is both "yes" and "no" with regard to teaching the arts.

For purposes of this essay, "the arts" are defined in the same manner as the National Standards define them, that is, as including the visual arts, music, drama, and dance. "Virtual schooling" is teaching and learning accomplished wholly or in significant part by means of electronic communication, rather than traditional face-to-face instruction. "E-learning," "e-teaching," and similar terms also incorporate some form of electronic communication; the prefix *cyber* attached to any root implies the use of the Internet. Indeed, the Internet plays a central role in all forms of virtual schooling today, unlike in the past when distance learning was conducted by other means, such as through correspondence, using audio- and videotapes, by telephone, and so on.

Communication between and among students and teachers is at the core of teaching and learning in schools. Whether schools are traditional or "virtual" is less important than whether such communication is effective. In addition, the arts are among those disciplines in which movement and multisensory interaction play significant roles in both teaching and learning. Educators and policy makers must consider how e-teaching and e-learning may be reasonably applied to the arts. Will electronic communication improve or diminish arts learning experiences and the acquisition of skills and knowledge? How will virtual schooling address the need for movement and multisensory interaction?

Three viewpoints for considering e-teaching and e-learning in these ways are to examine virtual schooling that 1) supplants, 2) augments, or 3) enriches traditional forms of teaching and learning. Education policy makers must take into account these kinds of considerations in order to frame the salient concepts to inform praxis.

Supplanting the Traditional

At the outset, it is impossible to argue for virtual schooling that *wholly* supplants traditional teaching and learning in the arts. Consider, first of all, that teachers cannot effectively teach pottery-making or dancing simply by telling students to look at a website or a video or some other two-dimensional communication form. The arts require multisensory instruction with particular attention to the tactile and the kinesthetic. Students will not learn to throw pots without getting their hands in the clay or to paint without picking up a brush. Dancers will not learn to dance by staring at a computer simulation or e-chatting with their instructor. They must get on their feet and move. Teaching and learning in the arts involve "real" doing — handwork, footwork, bodywork. A crucial element in this doing is the dynamic *physical* interaction of teacher and student, which cannot be accomplished electronically. The young violinist needs a teacher's hand to correct his or her fretting and bowing, not a picture or a video, however clever the simulation.

At the same time, there are *some aspects* of the arts that are not concerned with making and doing. In other words, there are the so-called academics of the arts: reading, viewing, listening, responding, writing — not moving and manipulating. And so, the next reasonable consideration becomes, Can these aspects of traditional schooling in the arts be supplanted by virtual schooling? Can virtual schooling be employed, for example, to teach art history or music history? Can it be used to teach aesthetics or criticism? To answer these questions, it is necessary to consider how these aspects of the arts are traditionally taught. The media of instruction are an entry point. If one can acquire the skills and knowledge necessary to comprehend art history solely from books, then what difference does it make whether the books are paper or electronic? Books are, after all, "virtual," merely *representations* of reality.

For example, how do students typically study Picasso's *Guernica*? If instruction proceeded only from a verbal or written description, it would not be judged adequate. A description, regardless of how detailed, can give only the most rudimentary sense of this monumental mural or of any other artwork. In traditional classrooms, therefore, students are given not only a description but also a visual representation: a photograph in a textbook, a slide, or a poster. Black-and-white photography gives at least the sense of any artwork; color photos represent them better. Even so, photographs are quite limited representations. They cannot convey the size (scale) of the work (certainly not in the case of Picasso's mural, Michelangelo's Sistine Ceiling, and so on) and they can only hint at texture. Despite these limitations, traditionally they have been judged to be adequate for the study of this Picasso painting and artworks in general. After all, it would not be reasonable for most students to travel to the Reina Sofia Museum in Madrid, Spain, to study the mural firsthand. Students might do so to research a thesis or dissertation but hardly for an undergraduate art survey, much less for a high school art class.

Thus an aspect of this consideration can be laid to rest. The media of virtual schooling can reasonably supplant traditional media by trading books, slides, and posters for electronic images on CD-ROMs or the Web. And the trade-off works to neither advantage nor disadvantage. Representations of artworks in books or online run the same gamut from poor to excellent quality. They are still merely representations. And accompanying texts are similarly varied. A case might be made that, in some instances, there are more available texts online than might be readily accessible in print in a given school or community. However, online textual information is not necessarily vetted by authority and can be unreliable. In addition, online information often is ephemeral, whereas texts in other forms (print, microfilm) may be more consistently available over time.

What About Human Interaction?

The real issue is not media or their availability, but human interaction between and among students and teachers. Set aside the media element and the fundamental question must be, Can the electronic communication of virtual schooling adequately substitute for the face-to-face communication of traditional schooling?

Early forms of distance learning substituted written for verbal interaction. For example, students taking correspondence courses wrote letters to their instructors (along with their assignments), and their instructors wrote back. For limited purposes, this form of teaching was judged to be adequate. However, no one would suggest that the *quality* of the distance learning experience was comparable to attending classes on campus. It served other purposes, a primary one being to bring otherwise unavailable education to geographically remote areas. With the development of advanced communication technology, distance learning programs adopted more sophisticated means of connecting students and teachers, such as two-way video, which allows students to interact with one another and their instructor in real time even though they are physically distant. In other words, the realism of the simulated "classroom" improved with the use of new technology. The closer the simulation is to the real thing, the better the quality of the human interaction of teaching and learning.

"Distance learning" has become "virtual schooling." The change in terminology reflects the advances in technology. Today's communications media can effectively simulate the visual and verbal components of the interactive environment of the traditional classroom. At least some forms of virtual schooling come close to creating the experience of a real classroom. But are they close enough? And is the most advanced technology available to most virtual schools?

The common virtual school model is one student-one computer, not one teacher and many students in many classrooms connected electronically for a close simulation of face-to-face teaching and learning. So the question to emphasize is the first, Can the one student-one computer cyber classroom create an instructional experience close to that of a real classroom?

Arts educators are not alone in considering this question. Dan Carnevale (2002), in an article titled "Virtual Faith," describes similar concerns raised at Eastern University in Pennsylvania, which offers a required Bible course online. Although the university encourages distant students to gather in small groups in their remote locations and to use e-mail and online chat rooms for discussion, officials worry that it may be impossible to meet the qualitative challenge of fostering the close relationships between faculty and students that characterize on-site education. Carnevale comments that "cyberspace offers no equivalent of the university chapel, no joyful hymns or moments joined in prayer" (p. A51).

On the surface, virtual schooling *can* supplant traditional schooling for certain types of arts classes. The classes are those in which 1) traditional and electronic media are comparable and interchangeable, 2) student-student and student-teacher interaction can reasonably be limited to the visual and the verbal (or written) without significantly diminishing the quality of such interaction, and 3) there is rich interaction among learners and teachers. Virtual schooling, given today's media, is an up-tick from the correspondence schools of old; but whether the improvement is significant or superficial remains dependent on the nature of the class and the intended outcomes of learning. In most cases, the utility of virtual schooling to supplant traditional schooling in the arts is severely limited.

Augmenting the Traditional

The next consideration is, To what extent can virtual schooling *augment* traditional schooling? While few opportunities exist in the arts to supplant traditional teaching and learning with e-teaching and e-learning, there are many ways that face-to-face teaching can be augmented by new media and communications technology.

Previously I cited the example of Picasso's *Guernica* and suggested that it probably did not matter whether students viewed the work in a book or online. Whether it concerns Picasso's mural or some other artwork, representations available in traditional sources can be supplemented by those found on CD-ROM or on the Internet. Similarly, online digital sampling can be used to augment resources in traditional music libraries. Indeed, the Internet is a trove to be tapped by all of the arts. Dance students will find websites of national and regional dance companies, performance schedules, and tour dates and venues in addition to equipment suppliers and other resources. Drama students will find similar performance websites, theater resources, and script services.

But the Internet also has limitations. As suggested, one is the question of authority. While a CD-ROM issued by a publisher may be as authoritative as its print counterpart, there is no guarantee that information placed online, whether by individuals or companies, has had any vetting unless it appears on the website of a recognized authority, such as a museum or archive. Additionally, there is the logistical problem now popularly called "link rot." Much of the content on the Web is ephemeral, likely to be found only as long as its originator keeps up the website. A recent article in *Education Week* referred to the Web as "the world's biggest piece of Swiss cheese: appetizing, but full of holes" (Trotter 2002, p. 1). Therefore, using virtual media to augment traditional sources forces teachers to reconstruct or at least to refresh their virtual materials regularly. And the problem of "dead" links is as frustrating for students as it is for teachers.

In addition to augmenting media resources, virtual schooling technology can supplement face-to-face communication by allowing students to communicate readily outside of class in chat rooms and by e-mail even when they attend the same school. Online study groups and one-on-one "e-tutoring" potentially can be as valuable to students as physically gathering to study together. And e-mail, which has some advantages over the telephone, has become an effective way for many teachers and students to stay in touch outside class times. Teachers and parents also stay in touch by e-mail and, in fact, are more likely to have greater contact than in the past, when staying in touch often meant trying to get parents to come to school or playing "telephone tag."

The technology typical of virtual schooling is particularly valuable to augment traditional schooling for special needs students. Students who need extra help for understanding subject matter will find multimedia through CD-ROM and Internet resources. Such resources can help students match their learning styles to the intellectual demands of their classes. Physically challenged students who find attending classes in the traditional manner daunting or impossible can be taught more effectively today than in times past by using innovative forms of assistive technology, such as voice-activated word-processors and audible output devices. (An organization that provides useful information and links is the Alliance for Technology Access at www.ataccess. org.)

Enriching the Traditional

As teachers and students explore the potential of virtual schooling strategies and technology, many are finding it possible to go beyond thinking of supplanting or augmenting traditional schooling. In terms of both media and communication, new technology is providing ways to *enrich* teaching and learning. For an example, it is useful to consider how computer technology is transforming visual arts education by reuniting art and science.

Albrecht Dürer, the German Renaissance master, created and used devices (technology) to assist with perspective, as can be seen in a number of his woodcuts. Leonardo da Vinci blended art and technology as often in painting as in mechanical invention. In fact, art and science were inextricably linked prior to Gutenberg, when, as James Bailey argues, "the printing press drove a five-hundred-year wedge between science and art, pushing the latter to the brink of extinction in the curriculum" (Bailey 1998, p. 17). Today the bits-and-pixels technology of the computer is bringing art and science back together in ways that can transform art education.

Computer technology is transforming the teaching of art through two types of activity: 1) using the computer to create or manipulate images and 2) using the computer to study the visual arts. The first involves art making, while the second involves art history, art criticism, and aesthetics, to use the components of discipline-based art education theory, or DBAE.

Student artists in today's classrooms already can use the computer to create plans for sculptures, ceramics, or other three-dimensional objects; to produce finished "virtual" works; and to render two-dimensional works. A student can make a sketch, for example, and electronically scan it to create a computer file. Then, using a program such as *Adobe Photoshop*, the student can manipulate the electronic image before taking it back to a paper printout to continue working by hand. Or the student can choose to refine the image wholly within the computer program. In the latter case, the finished work may simply be a computer file that can be viewed onscreen, or it may be printed out for a more traditional, "frameable" work.

The commercial art world is being transformed — indeed, already has been transformed — by these types of computer applications. For example, an illustrator preparing a book or magazine cover today may draft that image solely by using a computer. After submitting the image to an editor, suggested changes in textures, colors, or the placement of visual elements all can be effected electronically — without the old-fashioned necessity of recreating a paper-and-paint piece.

Computer-assisted art making has revolutionized commercial art and consequently is altering how art is taught to students who plan to enter that field. But computer technology also is changing the "fine" arts, as students explore alternatives to traditional methods of making art.

Computer technology also offers resources for teaching and learning about the visual arts. One form includes CD-ROM resources, many of which replicate but also enhance print resources. CD-ROM versions of print, from encyclopedias to art collections, offer students and teachers a wealth of information in a highly compact form. Typically, CDs also include audio and video, such as visuals of historic events, sound bites from famous people, and so on. These "extras," not available in print resources, enliven CDs. Students do not merely read the information, they experience it. No competent textbook publisher in art education today would consider offering a program without a CD component.

While most CDs cannot replace books that include in-depth information about art, often they provide highly accessible basic information. Moreover, because the best CD-ROM resources are interactive, they also motivate students to learn.

A second resource for teaching about art is connectivity to the Internet. School capacity for connectivity is increasing rapidly. Some 78% of schools were connected by 1997, according to the National Center for Education Statistics (1998). As connectivity extends into more and more individual classrooms, art educators and their students are discovering the burgeoning array of museums, galleries, archives, and libraries that maintain websites, which are continually being updated and expanded. Many websites also include lesson plans and samples to make teachers' work easier.

Connectivity is particularly important as art educators work to be responsive to cultural pluralism and diversity concerns. Teachers and students literally can explore the world's art online, and they can readily make connections between art and culture across national boundaries. Singly or in groups, they can embark on "virtual field trips" to hundreds of museums and galleries, including some that exist only on the Internet. For example, stu-

dents can take a virtual tour of the massive Louvre Museum in
Paris. Several "visits" will be necessary for the complete tour,
which is true of the real museum. Students even can combine art
and foreign language study by taking the tour in French, Spanish,
or Japanese, in addition to English. Smaller and closer to home is
the Andy Warhol Museum, physically housed in a converted
seven-story warehouse in Pittsburgh, Pennsylvania — and online,
where a floor-by-floor virtual tour is offered.

Ease of use and the wealth of resources also make the Internet
ideal for serendipitous teaching and learning, for capitalizing on
a teachable moment, and for nuturing creative approaches to art
history.

For example, not long ago I read a notice that the Italian government had rejected a request from the National Gallery of Art in
Washington, D.C., to bring the Bernini *David* to the United States.
The sculpture was to be the centerpiece of the gallery's celebration
of the 400th anniversary of Bernini's birth. However, Italian
authorities deemed the six-foot marble figure too fragile to travel.
Of course, few students would have been able to travel to
Washington to see Bernini's sculpture in any case; and far fewer
are likely to travel to Rome's Borghese Gallery to see the sculpture
there.

Apart from books, how might students discover (or be led to
discover) more about the *David* and its creator? Search the
Internet. A fascinating meander in cyberspace took me to "Thais
— 1200 anni di scultura italiana," or 1,200 Years of Italian
Sculpture (www.thais.it). Not only does this site contain numerous examples of Bernini's sculptures but, most important, it
contains the *David*. The famous statue is shown in both a full
view and a close-up of the head.

In an art classroom I might choose to project these views for
my students to study. A real-time projection could be created
using a minimum of equipment to display a life-size view of the
David. LCD projectors that interface with computers can display
large-scale images, and they are no more difficult to use than a
standard overhead projector. Eventually, in the wired classroom

of the future, they will be as common as the overhead is in today's classrooms.

I also could save the image as a file on my computer and then use it later in teaching a lesson. Or I could also print out a copy of the image on standard 8½" x 11" paper that could be duplicated as a handout.

By using a simple news item as a starting point, as in this example, a teacher (or an independent student) might embark on an Internet-based exploration that exemplifies the best character- istics of creative teaching and learning. And because the Internet knows no national boundaries, it is explicitly multicultural. In this example I was able to move easily among websites in the United States and Italy. Although some foreign sites require at least a rudimentary knowledge of the host language, many are available in multiple languages, English invariably being one of them.

This type of use, which certainly is not confined to the visual arts, goes beyond merely augmenting the traditional to truly enriching the teaching and learning experience.

Weighing the Pros and Cons

Education augmented or enriched by technology is not the connotation generally assigned to the term *virtual schooling*. True e-learning and e-teaching are embodied in the notion of sup- planting traditional face-to-face teaching with online education. The accepted sense of a virtual school is one in which instruction is delivered to a student working in some setting other than a school or classroom, usually at home, where the student is iso- lated from other students.

Much of the virtual schooling movement, if it can be so char- acterized, has come about in connection with home schooling. Virtual schools have emerged in the public school system as part of the school choice movement. These historical aspects of virtu- al schooling raise concerns in themselves, and those concerns can complicate the central concern of communication among and between students and teachers.

As virtual schooling has moved out of its initial base in high school subject matter, the concern about how students interact with one another and with teachers has increased. As Dennis L. Evans, director of programs for educational leadership development at the University of California, Irvine, put it, "One of the fundamental things elementary schools do is bring children together" (Galley 2003, p. 1). In the case of virtual schools, says Evans, "that entire major part of their education would be ripped away, and nothing would take its place" (p. 1).

This concern is especially pertinent in teaching the arts. While it could be argued that activities in the visual arts can be pursued individually, such is not the case with music, dance, and drama. Yes, of course, it is possible to learn to sing or play an instrument by oneself. A student can dance alone or learn a dramatic soliloquy without other students around. But for learning in music, dance, or drama to be fully realized, it must take place in a social context. Virtual music education can offer, at best, a watery, karaoke type of learning. What students need are opportunities to sing and perform with others. As for dance, it still takes two to tango. Drama cannot be effectively taught as monologue; students need to tread the boards, not just the keyboards. And there are compelling reasons why the visual arts also need to be taught at least partly in groups, a key one being that art itself always is viewed, understood, evaluated, and critiqued in societal contexts.

Even at the high school level, online education in the arts must be severely limited simply because most courses are designed to incorporate both a high degree of student-student and student-teacher interaction *and* hands-on activity, whether that means constructing a stage set, throwing a pot, dancing a pas de deux, or blowing a trumpet in a brass quintet. An examination of the list of arts courses in almost any high school will be telling. Although large schools have more options, small to mid-size high schools typically offer arts classes that *combine* making and doing activities with academic study (history, criticism, aesthetics). Because this "making" or "doing" is fully integrated with the elements that might be taught by electronic means, the majority of arts classes cannot be taught effectively solely through virtual schooling strategies.

The same contagious technophilia that gets an active 12-year-old to sit for hours playing computer games also infects educators, parents, and policy makers who see little difference between virtual schools and real classrooms. Undeniably the technology and learning strategies of online education can be valuable when used to augment or enrich traditional instruction. But virtual schooling, especially in the arts, is like armchair travel: nothing like being there. Not even close.

References

Bailey, James. "The Leonardo Loop: Science Returns to Art." *Technos* 7 (Spring 1998): 17-22.

Carnevale, Dan. "Virtual Faith." *Chronicle of Higher Education*, 22 November 2002, pp. A51-A52.

Galley, Michelle. "Despite Concerns, Online Elementary Schools Grow." *Education Week*, 8 January 2003, pp. 1, 12.

National Center for Education Statistics. *Internet Access in Public Schools*. Issue Brief. Washington, D.C.: Department of Education, Office of Educational Research and Improvement, March 1998.

Trotter, Andrew. "Too Often, Educators' Online Links Lead to Nowhere." *Education Week*, 4 December 2002, pp. 1, 15.

Life in the Cyber Trenches of the Virtual High School

Liz R. Pape

Liz R. Pape is chief executive officer at Virtual High School Inc., a project that received its initial funding through a grant from the U.S. Department of Education. VHS Inc., as it also is known, is physically located at 3 Clock Tower Place, Suite 100A, Maynard, MA 01754, and online at www.goVHS.org.

The fundamental aspects of a traditional classroom can be replicated virtually anywhere through online schooling. The Virtual High School (VHS), offering online education opportunities to high school students, transfers the elements of a traditional classroom to a virtual environment. Providing these online courses to high school students requires a breadth and depth of services similar to those provided by a brick-and-mortar high school.

Just as important as bringing elements of a classroom to the Internet is the training of the educators who will teach in these virtual classrooms. Since 1996 VHS Inc. has been working to provide appropriate online professional development to prepare teachers to teach online. In that time we have learned 1) how critical are standards in online course design and delivery, and 2) about the need to provide an infrastructure to support online course delivery to students. Along the way there have been unexpected developments and even minor catastrophes. Now — as I write this we are in the middle of our sixth school year of offering online courses — our philosophy has matured, and our course quality reflects that. At times during those six years we were in control of the improvement process, and at other times we arrived at a point not quite sure how we got there. The result has been an international collaboration of high schools offering online courses to their students, giving students opportunities to take courses not usually available to them and to participate in online classroom experiences in a global learning community.

In his graduation speech, Jason Wilcoxon, one of our 2002 professional development graduates, expressed his hopes for his students:

> I'm excited that my kids in a small urban school are going to, for a while, rise up above their surroundings. They'll get to see classes which have nothing to do with state mandated testing. They'll get to experience the kind of technology normally reserved for their suburban counterparts. They'll get to deal with what computer crashes are like. They'll fall behind. They'll get ahead. Most of all, though, they'll learn from someone completely outside of their reality. They'll learn about different people, and from different people. Hopefully, their classmates will learn from them.

Writing online course documents is not a walk in the park, especially when you spend time thinking through effective online pedagogy and then wringing out all that you can from the courseware to make sure it supports the pedagogy. Curriculum is just the first step, followed by thinking about online classroom features and community building — and those are just the elements of the courses. Next, you'll need to determine how to build an effective learning infrastructure around those courses. You'll need a grading system, registration system, online course catalog, technical infrastructure and support, and a course delivery monitoring system, as well as a way to keep it all secure from hackers, outages, and random acts of revisions by your software developers. Then there's the portal: the front page of your website and the front door to your school. Once people are in, where do they go?

Right to the classrooms? Are there other options, such as a virtual teacher's lounge or a showcase where you display awards and exemplary work?

This essay takes a journey through the cyber-trenches of a Virtual High School by examining the history of VHS Inc.

Origins of Virtual High School Inc.

Virtual High School Inc. is a nonprofit collaborative of high schools working together to offer full-semester online courses to high school students. Each school within the cooperative frees up one teacher for one period a day to teach a VHS course online. In exchange, that school receives 20 student seats in both the VHS fall and spring semesters. With these 20 seats each semester, 40 students at each local school may take any course in the VHS catalog, which currently includes nearly 120 courses. Through participation in VHS, schools expand the innovative, high-quality course offerings available to their students — courses that they might not otherwise have the staff to offer or enough students interested in taking.

VHS originally was funded under the U.S. Department of Education's Technology Innovation Challenge Grant. As part of the grant, SRI International conducted evaluations and research, which are available on our website. However, what has happened on a day-to-day basis often has been as compelling as our more formal reports.

Teacher Preparation and Online Course Design

Some of the questions that currently are being asked and answered by online course developers are: How do you build online courses that maintain the best features of face-to-face classes while taking advantage of the new medium in which they are being designed and delivered? What features from face-to-face classroom instruction should be retained? How do you integrate your course design philosophy with the courseware features? These same questions faced VHS when it began.

When VHS started, our courseware platform was not completely developed; yet we needed to begin training our teachers to teach online in order to meet our grant schedule and goals. As a result we were forced to focus on developing our online course pedagogy as we worked with our first group of teacher trainees. We did that without much knowledge of the features and capabilities of the courseware platform. Our online professional development was about teaching, not about the technology of the courseware. As we discussed what features from face-to-face teaching were critical elements in online courses, we refined our definition of good course design, absent the courseware.

Once the courseware became available for use, with a clear vision of how our teachers should teach online, the task of using the courseware for course development actually became easier than if we had started training our teachers on the courseware right from the start. As a result of the "problem," even after seven years of VHS online professional development, we still start our training with community building and collaboration.

Teachers as Students

Our teachers start as online students in their online professional development course. We begin with icebreaker activities as part of building online community. As they get acquainted with one another online, we involve them in group projects and team-building activities. These assignments are built around readings and discussions on collaborative learning, curriculum standards, assessments, and course design standards. Because teachers are accessing and interacting in their course in the same way as their high school students will, their focus is on learning in an online environment. They focus on the importance of student-centered learning, high levels of interaction and discussion among online students, and collaborative activities that use the medium effectively to transcend time and place. This philosophy of collaborative, student-centered learning remains a vital part of our course design and is reflected in our course design standards and course delivery. Teachers are given opportunities to reflect on these teachings and to discuss how these elements and lessons will affect their online teaching. Not surprisingly, over the years many also have put some of these lessons into practice in their face-to-face classes. Deborah Baker, a VHS teacher, commented:

> Having worked this year developing my course, I have grown in more ways than I can explain. It's not just that I have had to learn a whole new virtual world (including *Lotus Notes*); it's that being involved in long-distance learning has heightened my awareness of all aspects of my face-to-face teaching. For example, I work harder to clarify directions. I try to find new ways to connect with students and families. I am more inclined to encourage my students to use technology to solve problems and find information simply because I am more and more comfortable and confident with it myself. I shouldn't say "simply"; there's very little about this kind of learning that is simple — except for the fact that it is so exciting and powerful. And people who say it is impersonal haven't experienced what I have. . . . Being a part of a virtual community is as dynamic — though not visually — as is being a part of any group of people who share common goals/interests. . . . Simply know that I've loved being a part of VHS.

Real Teachers Develop Real Courses

During our first online professional development course in mid-1997, we received our beta version of the course-authoring platform. It was with this software that our first group of 28 teachers wrote their online VHS courses. Our teachers write all VHS courses during training. During that first professional development course, we were all new at learning the software — our training facilitators were barely a chapter ahead of the teachers they were training on the software.

As we learned the platform, we discovered bugs in the software or features that were written for corporate training needs that did not meet educational needs. Working with a beta version actually gave us an unanticipated advantage: The company's software developers were interested in learning from us and hearing our concerns as the courseware was put to use. We were able to work with their software developers so that future versions of the platform would better meet our needs.

Over time many companies have shifted their emphasis from virtual education to corporate training, a more lucrative market. This puts educators at a distinct disadvantage. As schools feel more pressure to produce results based on high-stakes testing, and as budgets and resources diminish during hard economic times, online education offers great opportunities to increase course offerings at schools. Online education can provide specialized courses to meet individual student needs and achieve economies of scale by pooling teacher resources and student needs through the Internet. However, if we are forced to use a course-authoring platform not designed for educators' needs, many online learning advantages will be outweighed by the disadvantages of an ineffective authoring tool. Educators must work together to create a market large enough that vendors will listen and respond when designing a course-authoring platform — and offer it at a price that school systems can afford.

Pedagogy Versus Course Software: Lessons Learned

As we worked through our first year of professional development for our VHS teachers, we slowly shifted our emphasis from pedagogy to course design. During the last half of our online professional development, our teachers wrote their online course documents, trying to write a full-semester high school course that they would teach the following semester. Our role as training facilitators was to continue to stay ahead with the software, learning how the features worked so that we could help our teachers as they used the software in writing their courses. Interestingly, during that first year, as we focused on learning the software, we lost sight of a key goal: VHS is about education, not technology. We continued to pile on more lessons about the features of the software.

To say that some of our teachers were overwhelmed would be an understatement. We also overwhelmed ourselves because we were not prepared for the technical support questions that would be generated by our technical lessons. Our teachers became increasingly frustrated, as did we. Some got so bogged down in the intricacies of the technology that they did not finish their courses in time for the start of the semester. However, because we had no review process in place to ensure that all courses met our standards, we trustingly started our first semester of delivering courses to VHS students with a range of courses in various stages of completion.

VHS Doors Open for the First Time

In September 1997 VHS started its first school year with 28 new VHS teachers, 28 new online courses, and about 400 students enrolled in VHS courses. We had students from Massachusetts, Pennsylvania, New Jersey, North Carolina, New Mexico, California, Washington, and other states. Our students' local schools ranged from urban to rural, large and small, from high-poverty to medium-wealth, and from high-minority populations to 97% white. It was an amazing microcosm of American schools. They were all at our online doorstep, waiting for the bell to ring and classes to start. When the bell rang, classes did start — and then proceeded to halt as the servers crashed. We rebooted the servers, and they crashed again; and so we rebooted, and they continued to crash. We could not keep classes in session. Students became frustrated, teachers were requesting more technical help, we were overwhelmed with trying to keep students and teachers supported, and still we could not figure out why the servers were crashing. We realized that no one had ever given us any data on server needs for online courses because there were no data to give. We were on the cutting edge.

Students were dropping out, afraid for their grade point averages. Teachers still were making lots of requests for technical support. We were running around, adding more capacity to our servers. Finally, Digital Equipment Corporation donated an industrial-strength server to VHS. At last, classes were back in session. Those students who had remained with us during that month of inactivity began participating in their online courses, and we breathed a sigh of relief.

Then, suddenly, a new issue arose. We were hearing concerns from students — some were even rebelling in their online courses. Why? A variety of reasons: Some VHS teachers were not responding to their students' questions, others were not giving students feedback on submitted work, others did not have lesson plans written into their course documents — in other words, students were coming to class, but some of the teachers were absent. We began communicating with the teachers, determining whether technical issues were preventing them from teaching. Sometimes that was the case, other times not. Sometimes the teachers just did not know our expectations for their online teaching behavior. We had not been clear enough during the professional development course about our expectations once they began teaching in VHS. Not only that, we had not been clear enough among ourselves — we had no process or procedures in place to monitor the quality of course delivery.

From that first year we learned some critical lessons and have since developed policies, processes, procedures, and standards to address those shortcomings.

Defining Standards

Assuming that you agree that online courses should be student-centered, have an appropriate level of student-student and student-teacher interaction, foster team building, include group projects in a collaborative learning environment, and use the medium to transcend time and place, how do you translate those ideas into course design and delivery standards? During our first year of course delivery, we realized how critical it was for us to answer this question and to put into place such standards and the means to ensure that they are met by all VHS courses and teachers.

Our first task was to define the standards. We began by convening a group of outside experts to assist us. We asked university distance learning faculty, state K-12 curriculum and instruction directors, and national education policy makers to become members of the VHS NetCourse Evaluation Board. The task of the NetCourse Evaluation Board was to become familiar with VHS online course design and then to bring their expertise into a discussion about VHS design and delivery standards, assisting us in writing those standards. After two days of face-to-face meetings and presentations and several months of online discussions, review, and revisions, the standards were published on the VHS website. VHS staff then used those standards to define the process and procedures we used to ensure VHS courses met those standards.

The standards affected VHS professional development courses and VHS delivery. We realized how closely both needed to work together. What staff members learn about teachers and courses while in delivery affects what is in our VHS professional development modules. Technical support needs are affected by both VHS professional development and delivery standards. Monitoring the quality of courses in delivery is affected by the quality of the courses and teachers that graduate from VHS professional development courses.

Monitoring Course Quality

With VHS design and delivery standards in place, we began to tighten up the online course design and delivery process. All VHS courses are evaluated several times while in development, culminating in semester-long courses that meet all VHS design standards prior to the teacher graduating from our online professional development courses. Delivery standards that address expectations about online teacher standards during course delivery are clearly communicated to the teachers as part of their professional development. Professional development facilitators are monitored to ensure that they are modeling the standards they are taught. All

VHS teachers are assigned an online mentor during their first semester of teaching. All VHS courses are monitored and evaluated weekly during their first semester of delivery. Based on that evaluation, courses and teachers are placed in one of two levels of monitoring. Those courses and teachers that do not meet all of the VHS standards for delivery continue to work with their mentors to achieve the standards. Those that have met the standards continue to be monitored to a lesser degree during subsequent semesters of delivery.

Standards are an integral part of how we maintain online course and teacher quality. By understanding the standards that are used in course design and delivery, consumers and purchasers of online courses can judge whether a course is of high quality. VHS has worked with the National Education Association and other national policymaking groups to publish a set of standards that can be used for this purpose. These standards are published on the NEA website at www.nea.org/technology/onlinecourse guide.html.

VHS Support Structure

Online courses, both their design and their delivery, are only a piece of the picture. What additional services need to be provided to support online courses, and who is responsible for providing those services? VHS Inc. is not a school but a nonprofit organization that provides the administrative, management, training, technical, and delivery services that allow member high schools to offer online courses to their students. We have put into place the systems that allow students to register for courses online and to receive grades securely online. We offer technical support to students and teachers and build a community among the member schools, teachers, and students. We also are responsible for ensuring that servers are up and running so classes are always available, making sure no unauthorized people are entering classes and gaining information about students or teachers, and ensuring that teachers are in classes and working appropriately with students.

Although VHS is not a school, our online presence resembles a school's physical presence. The VHS website is the access point for students and teachers entering their online courses. It includes additional services found in traditional schools, such as course registration, grading, a catalog of courses offered, and a faculty lounge. It also includes some not-so-traditional offerings, such as online course evaluations and a knowledge base for online help. Over the years we've realized how critical this online presence is, not only in facilitating online course delivery, but also in building community among all VHS teachers and students. While effective course design can build community within an online course, an effective online portal can build community among all members of the VHS community.

Opening Doors

Just as a traditional school has visitors in the main office, we occasionally get visitors knocking on our office door. Our online presence includes both public and private areas so that students, faculty, and staff remain safe and secure and yet visitors can get the support they need. We have many security measures in place within the private areas of our site. For example, students can access only the courses for which they are registered. Teachers can post grades only for the courses they are teaching. Logs are maintained of student and teacher access to courses.

At the same time, we welcome visitors who want to learn more about online education to the public face of our website. Our site has become a gathering place for those interested in learning more about online professional development and education. Unlike a traditional school, our online presence provides a way for us to safely and securely open our doors to all who have an interest in education, regardless of their geographic location, and to share our experiences of life in the cyber trenches of the Virtual High School.

Quality Control in Online Schools

Andrew A. Zucker

Andrew A. Zucker is associate director of the Center for Online Professional Education at the Education Development Center (EDC), a nonprofit research and development organization. This essay is based in part on reports prepared by SRI International for the Virtual High School evaluation and on The Virtual High School: Teaching Generation V, *published by Teachers College Press in 2003.*

Beginning in 1996 a team at SRI International studied and evaluated the Virtual High School in Hudson, Massachusetts, over five years. VHS, conceived and operated by the Concord Consortium and the Hudson Public Schools, was one of the first and has been one of the most successful virtual high schools in the United States. VHS Inc. (www.goVHS.org) is now an independent, nonprofit organization based in Maynard, Massachusetts, with participating schools in more than half of the states in the United States and in about a dozen foreign countries.

The SRI team analyzed surveys from thousands of students, teachers, principals, and other administrators; made multiple visits over five years to more than 10 regular public schools participating in VHS; convened an expert panel to review online courses in detail; interviewed dozens of people, including leaders of many other online schools; and reviewed much of the existing research about virtual learning. Several special studies were conducted by SRI, among them a matched comparison of face-to-face and VHS courses, which included a comparison of "key assignments" in both types of courses, and an online assessment of students designed to understand the effect of virtual courses on students' reasoning skills in a technological environment. Dr. Robert Kozma and I co-directed this five-year evaluation, which was published in a series of reports and finally in a book about VHS published by Teachers College Press.

Lessons Learned

The major finding of five years of investigation is simple and powerful. As we wrote in our book:

> VHS constitutes an authentic success story, when success stories about innovation are still rare in education, and it provides us with lessons learned that others can use as they venture into the world of virtual education. (Zucker et al. 2003, p. 15)

Success for the Virtual High School can be defined in many ways, most notably the fact that students are able to enroll in high-quality courses not otherwise available to them in their regular, brick-and-mortar schools. There has been a high degree of satisfaction among all participants; many students, teachers, and schools have been willing to sign up for more; and there is a demonstrated willingness on the part of schools to pay for VHS services. Importantly, VHS has proved to be a model for many other online schools, even in the for-profit sector.

All virtual schools are not the same. They differ in the types of courses offered, the role of the teachers, who awards credit, and in other dimensions. The VHS "model" is based on a consortium of schools that work together to offer a wide variety of online courses, with schools typically offering one course. In the main, the VHS courses have been one-semester offerings, repeated in the fall and spring. Students generally enroll in one or two VHS NetCourses (online courses) each year but continue to take most of their courses face-to-face in a regular school — an approach shared by many other online schools. Two other features of VHS that are increasingly being copied by other online schools are the requirement that participating schools have an on-site coordinator to help the VHS students and teachers and the requirement that participating teachers and site coordinators successfully complete an intensive online training before becoming active in VHS.

We have identified a number of important lessons from SRI's five-year evaluation. The first is that a virtual high school can be successful. Lesson number two is that the involvement of local site coordinators, as well as careful preparation of the teachers and coordinators, will contribute in important ways to an online school's success.

Many groups are learning, as we have, that online schools have real limitations. For example, students in virtual schools have fewer supports available to them than do students in brick-and-mortar schools, thus demanding greater independence on the part of the students. As a result, even though virtual schools may screen prospective students carefully, the dropout rates in online courses are higher than in face-to-face courses. Often, the "stopout" rates also are higher, meaning that some students who have not technically dropped a course do not work hard enough to earn a good grade.

Another of the limitations is today's Internet technology. Remarkable as it is, the Internet still is based primarily on text, presenting a significant barrier to students who are not fluent in reading and writing. The software used to access online courses typically makes it difficult to include people in online courses (such as parents or outside experts in a field) who are not actually enrolled in the course. And the Internet is not well-suited to certain types of courses, such as those that require laboratory equipment, oral conversation, or inspection of physical objects. Such limitations create difficulties for virtual high schools that will be overcome only slowly, as technological limitations are reduced by the evolution of the Internet.

Another lesson has emerged from the SRI evaluation and from other research: The promise that online schools will cost less than regular schools is, at best, premature. This is true especially in the case of students enrolled mainly in face-to-face courses in regular schools, supplemented by a few online courses, because the costs of virtual courses are then "add-ons" to the cost of regular schools. Yet, for most students who take an online course, this approach (maintaining a schedule combining regular and a few virtual courses) is probably the best one.

Many of the other lessons learned from the evaluation concern how to maintain high quality in the individual courses and in an online high school as a whole. As a leader of another virtual high school told us, ensuring high-quality instruction online is "what keeps me awake at night." Quality control should be a central concern for all online schools, and VHS has spent a lot of time and energy keeping its quality high.

Quality Control

Online schools require attention to a host of details — from which technologies to use, to the selection of courses to include in the catalog, to the roles of the teachers and ways that credit is awarded to students. There is no single key to success. Understanding the complexity of virtual schools and what that implies for quality control is essential.

It is not difficult to identify dozens of quality control procedures that are important for virtual schools. Following are seven important approaches that have been used successfully by administrators of the Virtual High School:

Professional development for teachers. Enrollment in the Teachers Learning Conference (TLC), a 26-week online professional development course, is a requirement for all new VHS teachers who plan to develop and offer a NetCourse. By becoming students in the medium, these teachers learn firsthand what their students will face. Experienced online instructors offer information and assistance on a wide variety of topics that are essential to online teaching. Those who do not learn how to use the online medium effectively enough to persuade the instructors that they will be good VHS teachers will "wash out" and not be allowed to offer an online course. The teachers who do make it usually find the work rewarding but demanding, and the great majority have chosen to offer their courses for years at a time.

Reviews of online courses prior to their first offering. One goal of the TLC is to help prospective VHS teachers develop Net-Courses that they will teach. Although a NetCourse typically is not completely finished by the end of the Teacher Learning Conference, VHS instructors and staff review it carefully. If too little progress has been made or if the course does not meet quality control standards, it will not be part of the VHS course catalog. Each year, a number of developing NetCourses are not ready to be included in VHS.

Faculty advisors. From the outset, having access to all the password-protected sites, VHS staff observed the NetCourses in action. It is possible to do the equivalent of a classroom observation by monitoring the teacher's and the students' postings online. As the number of VHS courses grew, it became apparent that the staff could not effectively monitor all of the NetCourses, so a set of positions was created for faculty advisors. These advisors serve somewhat the same role as department chairs in high schools, with particular emphasis on being sure that the NetCourses in a given field (mathematics, say) are of high quality. The faculty advisors are paid to provide regular feedback to VHS teachers, especially first-time teachers, based on observations of their NetCourses as they are being offered.

Written agreements with schools. VHS requires that schools satisfy certain minimum requirements, such as having appropriate technology in place for students to use when they take the VHS courses. Putting the agreements in writing and insisting that they be signed by the district's superintendent suggests that the agreements are important. In addition to promising to have in place the minimum technology requirements, participating schools need to agree to a variety of other conditions, such as to provide 20% release time for a local VHS site coordinator, pay for the VHS teacher and site coordinator to participate in online training courses, pay for books or other materials that students in other schools are required to use for the NetCourse taught by the VHS teacher at this school, and returning to VHS at the end of each semester all materials and books that have been sent to the school and used by VHS students for NetCourses they have taken during that semester.

Online preparation of students. Adults sometimes assume that all young people know how to use computers and the Internet effectively and efficiently. However, few students come to a virtual high school having had experience with online courses. As a result, VHS has found it important to provide students with an online orientation module when they are beginning. Students learn how to operate in the specific structure of the VHS online courses (for example, which on-screen buttons to click to access parts of the course, such as the threaded discussions or collections of online documents), how to upload homework, etiquette when communicating online, and tips for being effective when enrolled in a virtual course.

Parental notification. If students are doing poorly, VHS notifies the parents that there is a problem. Procedures also are in place for reporting midterm grades and for reporting and resolving problems. It is important to involve the site coordinator in the local school as well as to notify the parents if a student is doing poorly because parents are not easily able to monitor their child's online VHS work (which is password-protected) and do not routinely interact with the VHS teacher.

Training and use of site coordinators. Like the VHS teachers, new site coordinators are required to take an online course that helps prepare them for their new responsibilities. By acting as advisors and advocates for students and as local partners for the remote VHS teachers, the coordinators can solve problems that otherwise might become more serious. The quality of students' experiences has turned out to be related, in part, to the presence and the quality of the local, on-site coordinators.

In short, we have learned that few procedures in online schools can be taken for granted. Excellence is the result of a large number of well-conceived, well-staffed, and well-conducted activities. In order to help ensure that these efforts result in online learning experiences of high quality, a variety of groups, including VHS itself, has sought to develop standards of excellence.

Quality Standards

Prospective VHS teachers are introduced to written quality standards in the online course that they are required to take as preparation to teach in a virtual school. The standards used by VHS cover everything from the way that the teachers should use fonts and colors online to the nature of the course content and the way that it is organized in the virtual environment. VHS was among the first to develop standards. By now, several key organizations (including the National Education Association and the Southern Regional Education Board) have promulgated standards or policies related to high school online courses. Many of their documents, as well as those developed by VHS, can be found online.

One interesting set of standards for online courses developed by an expert panel focuses on four dimensions of course quality: curriculum content, pedagogy, course design, and student assessment (Yamashiro and Zucker 1999). Online courses vary in content as widely as do face-to-face courses in large high schools. However, according to the expert panel that reviewed a dozen VHS online courses in great detail, all online courses should have certain quality characteristics in common. Standards developed by the panel state:

- The course facilitates learning about important information, skills, and major ideas from multiple viewpoints.
- The course is designed to infuse critical thinking and problem solving.

- The materials, activities, and assignments are well matched to the capabilities of students and prerequisites are specified.
- Any controversial issues or materials are treated in a responsible manner.

In terms of pedagogy, virtual courses that simply provide a large volume of online text for students to read are not likely to be of high quality, nor are students likely to find them valuable. The expert panel determined that a high-quality online course conform to the following:

- The course encourages an active approach to learning the subject, including interaction with the teacher and other students.
- The course helps students make effective use of the online medium.
- The course integrates multiple methods of instruction, such as assigned reading, discussions, simulation, laboratories, assigned writing, critiques, peer review, and presentations.
- The course orchestrates discourse and collaboration among students.

The last is a particularly difficult goal to achieve in an online environment, and it takes a teacher skilled in the use of online pedagogy to reach this goal. Learning the necessary techniques to encourage students to interact and collaborate effectively online is one of the important reasons teachers need to study online learning before teaching in a virtual school.

Teachers must also make special efforts to be clear, specific, and engaging in an online course. The expert panel's expectations include:

- The course is structured in such a way that its organization, and use of the online medium, are adequately explained and accommodate the needs of students.
- All required course materials are made available to students, including some that may need to be mailed to them.
- The teacher clearly identifies performance objectives for students that are used to assess their work in the course.

- The structure of the course encourages regular interchange and feedback between student and teacher and guides students toward reflection on their own learning.

These standards, and several others developed by the panel, aim high. Many teachers of face-to-face courses would be hard-pressed to meet them. Yet that is as it should be, because virtual schools should not be held to lower standards than are regular schools. If they are, people will learn to look on them with suspicion. As an NEA technology brief on distance education suggests, distance education courses must be at least as rigorous as similar courses delivered by traditional means. Similarly, teachers of online courses should be highly qualified.

When teachers meet the standards for quality teaching online, the results are impressive. Reviewers said of one VHS course:

> The number and diversity of activities in the course designed to engage students actively in the substance of bioethics was very impressive: case studies, role playing, web searches, creating a logo and cartoon, surveys, persuasive essay writing, simulations of a national hearing, bioethics symposium presentations, creation of Web pages. The course design not only kept the course interesting and moving, but it also seemed to engage students in a way that kept them on schedule rather than falling behind.

Through the wide variety of quality control mechanisms identified above, as well as others, the expert panel convened by SRI found that VHS had achieved a high level of quality in its courses.

Need for Data on Virtual Schools

It is difficult for prospective students, parents, or others to "visit" online courses, as they might observe a face-to-face class or school. As a result, it is especially important that virtual high schools provide interested students and the public with pertinent information to help them judge whether the school and its courses will meet a particular student's needs.

A few online high schools have commissioned third-party evaluations. Besides the Virtual High School, the Florida Virtual School has commissioned and published the most extensive set of evaluation data (Bigbie and McCarroll 2000). Interestingly, the general conclusions about virtual schooling reached by the Florida Virtual School evaluators are similar to those reached by the SRI evaluation team. One hopes that policy makers and the public will conclude that the publication of such third-party data — or even reliable information gathered by the schools themselves — is an important piece of the quality control puzzle.

Parents and prospective students ought to have many questions. What is the nature of each course offered by a virtual school? What can students expect in terms of assignments, interactions with the teacher and other students, and time required to participate? What kinds of students are enrolled in the school, for example, by grade level or by geographic region? What are the dropout rates, either for individual courses or for the school as a whole? How many students have successfully completed each course?

A "consumer's guide" to online courses was published in *The School Administrator* (Berman and Pape 2001), providing another useful perspective for those interested in understanding what is needed to provide high-quality virtual schooling. And, as noted above, a variety of organizations publish standards and guidelines that are worthwhile for anyone, from a policy maker to a parent, who is interested in the quality of virtual schools.

Future of Virtual Schools

All signs are that virtual schooling is going to expand at a rapid rate. A dozen state-based virtual high schools already are operating, and the number is growing. Increasing numbers of students are also taking college and university courses online. The University of California system is beginning to provide high school students with access to Advanced Placement (AP) courses online, in part as a reaction to the fact that many high schools offer few, if any, AP courses. A surprisingly large proportion of the public accepts the idea that high school students may earn some of their credits online.

If the expected growth in virtual schooling does take place, it will be all the more important to keep an eye on quality. Good online teaching, a high-quality syllabus, and effective school administration are not simply the result of good luck.

Unfortunately, not all the virtual schools and online courses available now or coming tomorrow will provide a high-quality experience for students. Yet a great deal already is known about how to provide good courses, how to support students and teachers, and how to administer virtual schools effectively. Policy makers and the public must balance the need for experimentation with requirements and pressures for accountability, including truthfulness in advertising and in reporting data. If such a balance can be maintained, virtual high schools seem likely to become a significant part of the education system.

Resources

Berman, S.H., and Pape, E. "A Consumer's Guide to Online Courses." *School Administrator* 58 (October 2001): 14-18. www.aasa.org

Bigbie, C., and McCarroll, W. *The Florida High School Evaluation 1999-2000 Report*. Tallahassee: Florida State University, 2000. www.flvs.net/learn_more/surveys.htm

Yamashiro, K., and Zucker, A. *An Expert Panel Review of the Quality of Virtual High School Courses: Final Report*. Menlo Park, Calif.: SRI International, 1999. www.sri.com/policy/ctl/html/vhs.html

Zucker, A.; Kozma, R.; Yarnall, L.; Marder, C.; et al. *The Virtual High School: Teaching Generation V*. New York: Teachers College Press, 2003.

Appendix

Evaluating Website Content

Ellen Chamberlain

Ellen Chamberlain is director of the libraries at the University of South Carolina Beaufort (USCB). This essay is excerpted from her Phi Delta Kappa Educational Foundation fastback 492 of the same title, published in 2002.

On the Internet, anyone can become his or her own publisher at very little individual expense. All it takes is a "host" to provide server space and a URL (Web address). The Web is democracy in action; and it can be, and often is, disorganized and messy.

The Internet has been called an "electronic library." However, it bears scant resemblance to the traditional libraries we know so well. For starters, the "electronic library" has no comprehensive card catalog, no professional staff members on duty, and no procedures in place to screen acquisitions. Its virtual shelves are as likely to hold political tracts, advertising, conversations, cheap tabloids, pornography, hoaxes, and deliberate frauds as they are to have rational and serious works from reputable sources. All of its holdings are mixed together in no apparent order, and none of them are labeled. Most important, in the electronic library, there is no bibliographic control, that is, no way to freeze a webpage in time. Because of the dynamic nature and constant evolution of the Web, the page you cite today may be altered or revised tomorrow, or it might disappear completely. The page owner may or may not acknowledge any changes to the text and, if he relocates the page, he may or may not leave a forwarding address.

With all of these obvious negatives, why would anyone choose electronic formats over print? Wouldn't it be better to avoid the freely available digital information altogether? The answer is that, if we avoid the Internet, we would miss too much that is valuable. Instead, we need to train ourselves to look at online information with a critical eye. We need to take the responsibility to evaluate and screen what we find.

Criteria for Evaluating Webpages

Many librarians and other research specialists have created their own Internet sites to address the issue of evaluating information on the Web. Not all recommend the same criteria for evaluation, but their selections are similar in substance and intent.

I have selected the following criteria for discussion: purpose, authority, currency, content, and page design. It is not necessary to use them all at any one time. Choose only those that seem most appropriate for your current needs and search situation.

Purpose

Your Purpose. Before you begin, take a moment to assess your purpose. Are you intending to argue a point, discuss a topic, show both sides of an issue, prepare a case for or against, explore a subject, answer a question, satisfy your curiosity, or just entertain yourself? Do you want to gather information about the threat of weapons of mass destruction or about the pros and cons of charter schools? Do you intend to debate the existence of global warming or examine the advertising techniques of pharmaceutical companies?

What are your needs and expectations? Spend some time thinking about the kind of page that would satisfy your needs. Are you looking for a quick overview, or do you require something with greater breadth and depth? Are you seeking a general explanation or a technical one?

Once you are viewing a page, ask yourself these questions: Does the purpose of the webpage fit my needs? Is it aimed at my level? Does it contain the type of information I am searching for at this moment?

Your answers will have a bearing on the outcome of your search. How you determine the quality of the pages you come across depends a great deal on how well they fit your purpose. The same page that would be acceptable as a source for a humorous speech might be totally inappropriate for inclusion in a serious paper. Once you are clear about your own purpose, it will be much easier to evaluate the webpages you visit.

Author's Purpose. Purpose refers to intent. Authors and sponsors of webpages aim to communicate something specific to a particular audience. They may create their pages to explain, inform, persuade, or promote. They may have a desire to rant, or even to play a trick or two on unsuspecting visitors. They could be filling their pages with exaggerations, distortions, and lies. You might have read about the webpage posted a few years ago promoting the Minnesota River in Mankato, Minnesota, as an ideal spot for whale watching. A quick look at any map should have alerted even the most "geographically challenged" folks that something was amiss, and yet the site still managed to fool a few people who made the trip to Mankato in vain.

Sometimes you can discern the purpose of a page by the tone of voice that is used. Is it formal, serious or scholarly, or perhaps informal, humorous, or ironic? Sometimes you can pick up clues from the text itself. Does the presentation appear to be straightforward and fair-minded, or can you detect a bias? Is the text believable, or does it show signs of parody or farce?

Think about the target audience. Is the vocabulary limited and the coverage slight? If so, the page probably was designed for children or young readers. Is it loaded with scientific or technical jargon? That page could be aimed at researchers and technical specialists. If you can determine the purpose of a page, as well as its intended audience, you will be better able to assess the reliability and suitability of the information on the page as it relates to you and your current needs.

Some website creators are very helpful in this regard. They include directional links to subpages titled "About Us" or "Our Philosophy." Others are less forthcoming. A few may have hidden agendas. They may be mixing facts with opinions in order to sell you something, win you over to their point of view, or just put one over on you for the fun of it.

In June 1997 Mary Schmich, a writer for the *Chicago Tribune*, penned a column that mocked traditional, stodgy commencement addresses. It began, "Ladies and gentlemen of the class of '97: Wear sunscreen . . ." Someone posted her column on the Web and attributed it to a commencement speech supposedly given by author Kurt Vonnegut at MIT. Within days, the column had been forwarded to email addresses around the world. It still is available on the Web and, in many cases, still is attributed to Vonnegut.

While you cannot always discern the author's purpose, it's important to try. In a serious paper, to unknowingly include references to webpages that turn out to be advertisements, spoofs, or frauds is embarrassing and dilutes the credibility of the entire work.

Watch for these red flags:

- Apparent bias in the text.
- A suspicion you are being manipulated.
- Incomplete or one-sided presentation.
- Distorted facts or exaggerated opinions.
- Tone of voice at odds with subject matter.

Authority

Authority refers to the individual responsible for the content on the page. In a high-quality webpage, the name of the author is clearly stated in a prominent place. If the author has an affiliation with an organization, it is noted.

Unlike scholarly books and journal articles, websites seldom are reviewed or refereed and normally do not contain introductory or author notes that would provide credentials. Therefore, if an author's name appears on a page, it should be followed by additional information, such as credentials or experience, that clearly supports the content and is verifiable.

The author also should supply a means for you to contact him, either through surface mail or an e-mail address. This does not always happen. E-mail addresses are easily falsified, as are credentials and statements of experience. Check both links and e-mail addresses to make sure they lead to authorized sources. If this is a content-packed page, the e-mail address of a webmaster, who is not the author, will not suffice; nor will addresses that turn out to be e-mail accounts freely available through commercial vendors and portals.

Of course, every individual who authors a webpage doesn't have to be a noted professional or a certified expert. He should not be averse, however, to telling you who he is and how he came by his knowledge. If what he says is legitimate, you will be able to verify it on other similar pages.

Verification of authority is especially important when the author lists no connection to any sponsoring body. Approach these pages with caution. They are most likely personal pages, created by individuals and hosted on the Web by an Internet service provider (ISP) for a monthly fee. The information they contain should be checked with other credible sources before you accept and use it.

Some pages do not list any individual's name as author of the textual material. In these cases, it is the sponsors — usually institutions, agencies, or business entities — that assume responsibility for the content. If they are well known to the public, they will have an established reputation on which you should be able to rely. If no sponsoring agency is listed or the name given is unknown to you, you'll need to look further to verify their authority.

One way to check authority is to see who is linking to the page from external sites, as well as what links are maintained by the page to other external sites. The links may be able to tell you a lot about the perceived quality of the page itself. Do the links connect to substantive sites that corroborate or add to the information you already accessed? Some search engines, such as Google, prioritize their retrieval lists based on link popularity: the more sites that point to a particular page, the higher that page's position is in Google's relevance rankings.

A page that lacks verifiable authority, either an individual author or a sponsoring agency, should be approached with skepticism. A few years ago, the *New Yorker* published a cartoon by Peter Steiner showing two dogs in front of a computer, with the one at the keyboard saying to the other, "On the Internet, nobody knows you're a dog." How true!

Watch for these red flags:

- Anonymous page author.
- Anonymous page sponsor.
- Inflated credentials (for example, title, education, experience, training) that lack authenticity.
- No credentials listed for author.
- Generic e-mail address for author that does not confirm authority claims.
- No provision for contacting author, through surface mail or e-mail, or by telephone or fax.

Currency

Currency refers to timeliness. It is reflected in the actual currency of the textual content and in the calendar updates noted on the bottom of the webpage. Checking the currency of webpages is important, though it is far from an exact science. No two sites approach currency in the same way. Some pages use dates to show the last time the links were checked. Others indicate the last time content was updated, while a few refer to the first time the page files were uploaded to the server. Then there are those that post no dates at all.

Of course, the more information that is provided, the more accurately you will be able to determine the currency of the page. However, even when dates are included, they can be ambiguous. A recent update may not ensure that the textual content is current but only that something on the page has been changed, for example, a misspelled word corrected or a typographical error fixed.

When it comes to the overall subject of currency, the Internet has a decided advantage over the world of print. This is mainly because electronic information can be created, updated, and disseminated in a matter of minutes, without having to wait for the next edition to appear days, months, or even years later. Currency becomes a very important factor when dealing with information in areas of rapid change, for example, when posting stock market quotations or late-breaking news. In fact, if you are unable to verify exactly when and how often pages such as these are updated, you had better not consult them.

Currency also is important when presenting information in the sciences, computer technologies, business, education, and the medical professions. All of these subjects depend on frequent updates and current news. On the other hand, the immediate availability of current information in the humanities (for example, literary criticism or historical analysis) may be less important.

Currency is one way to ascertain whether a page is continuing to be maintained. If there are numerous dead links, broken links, or empty files on a page, you may assume that it is unstable and would not be a reliable source. Page stability is especially important when you are writing a paper and using the Web for source material. Because websites are volatile and may be edited, moved, or deleted at any time, you need to pay close attention to the last update, as well as to the credentials and reputation of the page sponsor and author.

Always be sure to make and keep a backup copy (in print or on disk) of what you find on the Web. And be sure to record the date on which you found it. In this way, you will be able to verify your sources later on.

Currency on the Web cannot be taken for granted. You will find some pages unstable, changing without warning. Others that should be continuously updating their content may not change at all.

Watch for these red flags:

- No indication of last content update.
- No indication of last link update.

- Dates on page not current.
- Dead and broken links on page.

Content

Content refers to text. The content of a webpage may consist of both primary and secondary textual material. Briefly, primary material is original information (manuscripts and documents), while secondary material is information about information (reviews and commentaries). Both kinds of content may contain facts, opinions, advice, and arguments. These elements are not always easy to separate.

Since anyone can publish anything on the Web, you should not be surprised to find more personal opinion than fact. Also, be aware that many Web authors are adept at convincing you that their opinions are facts. However, facts can be verified. They can be demonstrated, observed, or confirmed by reputable sources. Opinions are harder to quantify. They may be based on sound logic, experience, or research or they may have been plucked from thin air.

Whatever the nature of the content, you will want to know where the author got his information. Does he help you verify the subject by providing links to source materials that support the text? If he cites statistics, does he point you to reliable sources?

Content involves many elements of language, including style, coherence, and correctness. Examine the text. Is it explicit and precise? Look for clarity of expression and usage that is suitable to the content of the page. Be alert to vagueness in writing style, the frequent use of sweeping generalizations, stereotyping, or an overriding concern with ethnicity. These are not good indicators of quality content. Serious works do not depend on emotional rhetoric or fuzzy logic. The style they use is professional, concrete, and direct. Look for proper grammar and spelling. Whether from ignorance or carelessness, textual errors say something about the writer, and it's usually not positive.

Be sure to look at how well the page covers your topic. If you intend to cite this information in a paper, you will want a page that consists of more than just a series of links to other pages (unless it's a bibliography). The page should be one that covers your topic to the expected degree of depth and breadth and at a level appropriate for your needs.

Finally, try to distinguish between serious content and promotion or advertising. This is getting harder to do, as more pages seek to cover expenses by incorporating commercial advertisements into their subject matter. Use your common sense. Is the page truly informational, or is it actually an advertisement masquerading as information? What would you think if you knew that the favorable Web review of the new textbook you were about to purchase was written by the publisher? Always approach Web content with a critical eye.

Watch for these red flags:

- Unsupported claims or claims too good to be true.
- Apparent bias in the text.
- Coverage that appears skimpy or slight.
- Pages that consist primarily of links to other pages.
- Obvious textual inaccuracies, bad grammar, or misspelled words.
- Emotional rhetoric.
- Absence of links to other sites for corroboration or further information.

Page Design

Page design refers to appearance and workability. Good design is essential to information retrieval on the Web. Without it, serious seekers may not stay around long enough to discover what the page has to offer.

As members of a consumer society raised in an advertising age, we ought to be pretty familiar with design methods and media. However, the Web continues to open up new and innovative avenues in the field of audio and visual design. Website developers have become adept at creating attention-getting pages out of a mixture of graphic art, hot links, image maps, forms, cgi-scripts, audio and visual clips, Java Scripts, and Java applets. Many of these innovations assist in the acquisition of information, while others, such as popup ads, flashing banners, and an overabundance of animated gifs (images), are downright annoying.

Commercial sites, now the fastest growing category of sites on the Web, are clearly the most adept at using layout and design elements. As with every innovation, however, some of them tend to go overboard, allowing "glitzy" graphics or multiple, slow-loading images to take complete control of their pages.

The best designs maintain a reasonable balance between image and text and do not require visitors to traverse several layers of pages before finally reaching the textual content. Good designs avoid jarring color schemes and busy, cluttered layouts. They make good use of white space, fonts, and type sizes to assist the user in reading the screens.

Well-designed websites ensure a fast response time and provide text-only options and other alternatives for users with special needs. They do not require special helper applications, plug-in software extensions, or the latest browser releases to view their pages. They usually mount an internal search engine on the home page so that users may search the entire site.

Well-designed websites also create internal and external directional pointers to help users find their way around. They provide clear, easy-to-navigate pathways connecting each of the content pages to every other page and back to the home page. This is an important feature because search engines and other hyperlinks often drop users down into the middle of websites, rather than at their home pages, where most site-based navigational tools are found. Without access to at least one of these directional tools (a table of contents, site map, search engine, etc.), it is difficult to figure out where you are, much less where you might wish to go next. When a site migrates to a new server, well-designed websites create external pointers to the new location.

Good page designs attract viewers and enhance the usefulness of websites. Poor designs turn potentially useful pages into sites that are virtually inaccessible to the general public.

Watch for these red flags:

- No balance between image and text.
- Inadequate or missing navigational links within website.
- Too many large images that load slowly.
- No allowances for variations in computers and levels of connectivity.
- Page organization that hinders searching.
- Cluttered, difficult-to-read screens.

Using Web Addresses for Evaluation

Information on the Web comes in a variety of forms. Not all websites have the same look, feel, or substance. Some are more reliable than others are. For example, the most consistently trustworthy sites on the Web traditionally have been those sponsored by major universities, research centers, and government agencies, all of which put their names and reputations behind their pages. The least trustworthy sites are those authored by individuals, without credentials, who have no connection to any known organization.

Obviously, it is important to determine webpage sponsorship up front, but how do you do that when the information is not readily available on the sites themselves? One way is to extract it from the Web addresses, or URLs.

The URL, which stands for Universal (or Uniform) Resource Locator, is the webpage address that appears in the address box at the top of each visited page. Knowing how to read URLs is important because they can tell you a lot about the page you are viewing. For example, here is the URL for Bare Bones, a search engine tutorial I created in January 2000:

http://www.sc.edu/beaufort/library/bones.html

This is what it means when you break it down, reading from left to right:

Protocol://server.domain/directory/sub-directory/filename.filetype

- "http" is the transfer protocol (type of information being transferred).

- "www" is the host computer name (or server name).
- "sc" (University of South Carolina) is the second-level domain name.
- "edu" is the top-level domain name.
- "beaufort" is the directory name.
- "library" is the sub-directory name.
- "bones" is the file name.
- "html" is the file type and, in this case, stands for hypertext mark-up language.

For the purpose of evaluating content, the most important part of the URL is the top-level domain name, which identifies the type of sponsor. Only a few top-level domains currently are recognized, but this is changing. The following is a list of the top-level domains established by Network Solutions Inc., which pioneered in the development of registering Web addresses by domain name:

.edu: educational sites, sponsored by colleges and universities. These sites may contain pages created by faculty and students, as well as "official" pages created and maintained by administrative offices within the institutions. Outside the United States, academic sites are identified by use of the ".ac" domain. Sites in the .edu and .ac domains are considered very reliable.

.com: commercial sites, sponsored by business interests. Commercial sites are the most numerous sites on the Web and the fastest growing as well. They include large and small businesses, commercial enterprises, individual entrepreneurs, and news media and entertainment outlets. They should be approached with caution because, while they are good information sources, the information they provide is usually one-sided.

.gov: U.S. government sites, sponsored by branches, agencies, and departments of the U.S. government. These are non-military sites. They are a good source for primary documents and current statistics and are considered very reliable.

.mil: U.S. military sites, sponsored by branches of the military. Many of these sites are similar to the ".com" sites in that they have their own agenda. Approach them with caution.

.net: networks, sponsored by Internet service providers, telecommunications companies, and networking organizations. This category includes commercial sites as well as personal pages that are authored by individuals who pay a monthly fee for the server space. These pages are not screened, so you should be cautious in their use.

.org: U.S. professional and nonprofit organizations and others, sponsored by a variety of sources, including individuals. This category is home to many "advocacy" sites that are openly one-sided and created to influence public opinion. Approach these pages with cautious skepticism.

An additional top-level domain name, the two-letter country code, is used routinely to identify countries around the world, for example, ".uk" for United Kingdom, ".ca" for Canada, and ".fr" for France. Because the Internet was created in this country, the two-letter code for the United States, ".us," was not assigned to the original list of top-domain names, though you see it in the URLs of state and local government hosts, including many public schools and community colleges (the latter also use the ".cc" or the ".edu" designations).

In mid-November 2000, the Internet Corporation for Assigned Names and Numbers (ICANN) voted to accept an additional seven new top-level domain suffixes, some of which you may already be seeing:

.aero: restricted use by air transportation industry.

.biz: general use by businesses.

.coop: restricted use by cooperatives.

.info: general use by both commercial and noncommercial sites.

.museum: restricted use by museums.

.name: general use by individuals.

.pro: restricted use by certified professionals and professional entities.

As the Internet grows, you can expect to see the number of top-level domain names grow as well.

Types of Websites

Website authors and sponsors create a variety of pages on the Web. The basic types include: commercial, advocacy, informational, news and journalism, personal, and entertainment. In your efforts to evaluate information quality, the criteria you select will vary according to the type of webpage you encounter.

Commercial Pages. Commercial pages are sponsored by businesses concerned with promoting and selling products. Commercial sites are the largest segment on the Web and are identified by the use of the ".com" domain in their URLs. Often they provide reliable information about their products while presenting useful tips in their areas of expertise. For example, manufacturers of carpeting and carpet cleaners are excellent sources for information on how to remove stains. However, do not forget that they are on the Web to make money.

When applying evaluation criteria to commercial pages on the Web, concentrate on examining content. Does the sponsor back up the claims with evidence? Are the claims reasonable and do they sound credible? Does the sponsor provide an opportunity for interactive communication with the public, so that individuals who have tried his product may respond to his promotions?

Advocacy Pages. Advocacy pages are those that exist to influence public opinion. They are found most often under the ".org," ".com," or ".net" domain names. Advocacy pages may be authored by individuals, but usually they are sponsored by organizations dedicated to one or more specific issues. Because they are focused on trying to sell their ideas to the public, advocacy pages are notoriously one-sided. Do not look for them to provide you with information on, or links to, opposing points of view.

This does not mean that advocacy pages have nothing to offer. On the contrary, they are very good sources of information. Their pages are usually heavy on content and contain archives or links to other background materials and articles that support their point of view. Of course, it is up to you to do the digging. Do not forget that you have to look further to get opposing arguments.

When applying evaluation criteria to advocacy pages on the Web, pay close attention to purpose and authority. Who is sponsoring the page, and might they have an ulterior motive? What is their experience and expertise in this field? Look also at content. Are the arguments reasonable and well grounded in known fact? Can they be corroborated?

Informational Pages. Informational pages exist to present factual information. They usually are sponsored by education institutions or government agencies and, not surprisingly, are located most often under the ".edu" or ".gov" domain names. Informational pages strive to maintain objectivity and, when dealing with controversial issues, will usually endeavor to present all sides of an argument.

When applying evaluation criteria to informational pages on the Web, examine authority. Since the name and reputation of the sponsors are closely tied to whatever information is presented on these pages, you need to know who is publishing or underwriting them. When research is presented on the Web, even under the ".gov" and ".edu" domains, it pays to ask just who is funding the research. You might discover that the informational page you are viewing is not quite as objective and unbiased as it appears.

On the Web, advocacy and commercial pages often masquerade as informational pages. How would you characterize, for example, a Pentagon-sponsored website presenting information favorable to the proposed Missile Defense System (MDS)? What would you think about a webpage sponsored by a major timber company that defines clear-cutting as a "best forestry practice"? Even with well-known and respected websites, you should try to determine any hidden motives.

News and Journalism Pages. Sponsored by major media sources (newspapers, television, radio, and magazines), news and journalism pages provide access to current and breaking news, archives of past news stories, online versions of popular journals, and current and archived columns written by reporters and freelance journalists around the world. News and journalism pages are part of the commercial sector and are located under the ".com" domain name.

When applying evaluation criteria to news pages on the Web, pay close attention to currency. This is the area where the Internet has a great advantage over print resources. Major media sources usually update their Web news pages by the hour or even more often. However, they also empty their archives frequently, which can become a problem if you are citing news articles in your research paper. Remember, always make and keep that copy.

With news and journalism pages, you should look at authority and purpose. Are the writers and publishers known for harboring a political bias, for example, a right-wing or far-left philosophy? Do they try to slant or "spin" the news in one direction or another? Of course, the suspected biases of certain news media outlets and individual reporters, whether substantiated or not, are legendary. You will need to corroborate your findings with supporting evidence from other sources.

Personal Pages. Personal pages are published by individuals who may or may not have some kind of affiliation with larger organizations or institutions. Personal pages can, and do, relate to every subject imaginable. They can be serious, informative, humorous, satiric, salacious, or even silly. Their informational content can be accurate and reliable or laced with falsehoods, fabrications, exaggerations, and downright lies.

Personal pages most often are found under the ".com" or ".net" domain names. This is because individuals must purchase server space to host their pages, and this space most often is available through commercial ISPs. Some personal pages can be identified by the use of the tilde (~) near the end of the URL address, indicating the presence of a personal directory on a larger server. Whenever you see the tilde, be aware that the information contained on that page is personal and may or may not represent the position of the sponsoring home site. This is the case with many personal pages created in the ".edu" domain by individual instructors and students at academic institutions.

Many personal pages can be compared to vanity press publications. They contain personal information, résumés, photos, and the like, and often are created for family and friends. However, a growing number have appeared in the past few years with a definite agenda and a political point of view. These pages are not recommended as sources for serious research unless their content can be verified by other reputable sources. Continue to check authority. Do the authors supply credentials to support their points of view? Can you verify these credentials in any way? Do they appear to know their facts, or are they publishing unsubstantiated opinion?

The most recent online status symbol involves purchasing and registering personal domain names. These names can take a multitude of forms, usually a version of an individual's family name, in which case they are easily recognizable. However, some individuals purposely select domain names that point to organizations and agencies with which they have no official connection. On the Web, it always pays to be alert.

Entertainment Pages. Entertainment pages are those that provide humor, games, puzzles, music, drama, or similar activities. Although some entertainment pages are personal pages created by individuals, more are sponsored by commercial interests trying to convince users to buy a particular product or service. They may offer special promotions and provide free, limited access to their software in order to entice users to return and eventually purchase the entire package.

Most entertainment pages carry the ".com" designation in their URLs. When applying evaluation criteria to entertainment pages, look first at the page design. This is a major component of entertainment pages. Poor designs will turn potential buyers or users away, very possibly never to return.

Conclusion

Every webpage has a point of view. Some websites exist to express the "official" line of their owners. These pages function within organizational or institutional settings where the information is filtered and controlled from the top. The sponsoring organizations may be commercial, educational, military, nonprofit, or professional; but they all share one thing in common: they do not stray far from the market-oriented script that promotes their own interests.

In a separate category, "unofficial" websites exist to provide a way for the individual, who could be anyone from the dissatisfied customer to the whistle-blower, to have his say. The Internet, because of its openness, provides a unique opportunity for the public to access so-called raw information that, due to publishing roadblocks and the excessive costs involved, might otherwise never make it into print. Sometimes, at these unofficial sites, you may obtain information that cannot be found any other way.

To point out that such pages require close scrutiny is probably unnecessary. But their very presence is a gift. It has been said that knowledge is power, and information is the raw material of knowledge. Certainly, those who control the flow of reliable information have access to a large part of the power that comes with knowledge. As long as all sources of information, official and unofficial, continue to be freely available on the Web, every one of us has the opportunity, however small, to share in both the knowledge and the power. That's the beauty of the Internet.